Dedication

This book would not have been possible without all the players and managers of the teams I had the privilege to play football for. Too many to mention you individually, so I'll just name the teams and trust that you know who you are. It was a pleasure playing with you all:

Fulston Manor
Swale Magpies
Borden GS
Sheppey United
Ealing CHE
Old Oak
FC Olympic
Teynham and Lynsted
Lotus Sports
Los Inútiles

Thanks for the memories.

CONTENTS

THE FORGOTTEN FOOTBALLER   PAGE 5

APPROACHING SILENCE   PAGE 94

BLUE-SKINNED GODS   PAGE 191

THE FORGOTTEN FOOTBALLER

ONE

It was kind of fitting that I should be making this journey by train. The same slow branch line that had taken me to the same destination all those years before. Things had been so different then, and it was almost impossible to believe that I was the same person. What had I been when I had made this journey for the first time? Just sixteen. So nervous about where I was going that my legs had been shaking uncontrollably since the moment the train had pulled out of the station. I also remember feeling very alone, scared almost, yes, definitely scared, perhaps terrified would be the word. I had been expecting my father to accompany me on this potentially momentous journey, but at the last minute he had told me, as we waited in the queue to buy tickets, that he just didn't have enough money for the two of us to go. He had waved me off from the platform shouting encouragement until he was left behind, and I was forced to face the world on my own for the very first time. I wonder what would have happened if my father had not been able to find the money for my ticket? I guess things would have turned out very differently, and perhaps that wouldn't have been such a bad thing.

So, here I was, making the same journey, but of course this time my legs weren't shaking, although, I must confess, that I was feeling just a little nervous. The train stumbled across the points taking it off the mainline, and we headed away from the town and into the country. I had the window right down so that a cool breeze would blow in from the fields, just as I had done at sixteen. The carriage, some relic from a bygone era, was empty and I was alone, but I had grown used to being alone. Seven years in prison was enough to make anyone feel alone, especially in the solitude of the night, when even my own skull had seemed like a prison for my brain. The most terrible thing about prison, apart from the terrible loneliness, was the time that you had to reflect on things. My life had gone into limbo from the first day I had been locked away, and all I had were memories from before, memories I picked over every night beneath the shroud of darkness that hung over my head. Sometimes, I would almost want to cry and on occasions I had even contemplated suicide as a way out. But, somehow I had managed to survive. And now here I was, a free man again at last. Not forgiven, just allowed out, the forgotten footballer.

The train slowed into the first station, Kemsley, and I remembered how, at sixteen, each passing station had increased my nerves, and how on crossing the Kingsferry Bridge onto the island I had almost vomited. This time the bridge came and went and I looked over the marshes with their tall reeds and cotton wool sheep, until another town crept into view. Queenborough signalled that the short journey was coming to an end, and once out of that small station we were already into the industrial outskirts of Sheerness. As the train came to a final halt, I closed my eyes, took a deep breath, and steadied myself ready for what was to come, just as I had done as a kid. My father had drawn me a small map of how to get from the station to the football ground, and I had clutched it tightly in both hands and set off walking. I didn't need a map this time, I knew the route well enough, even after all these years it was firmly engraved upon my mind. There are some things we never forget.

Coming out of the station, I turned right and then right again to walk back alongside the train tracks. I crossed a road as the tracks disappeared away towards the steel works and entered a housing estate. There was a big supermarket and, at the end of the car park, the road that led to the ground. I was surprised to find that there were new houses all around. It wasn't the rundown council estate it had once been, and I couldn't even see the floodlights. I walked on, slightly worried now, until I got to the place where I was sure the pitch should have been. Instead of the big red gates welcoming you to Botany Road the home of Sheppey United, there was a new row of houses. The fact that the road was now called United Close made me sure that I was actually in the right place, but now I went into a panic. Where were the big red gates? Where were the breeze-block changing rooms and the little corrugated iron-roofed stand? And the floodlights? What had they done with the floodlights? What had they done with Sheppey United? I turned full circle to make sure it wasn't just behind me or something, but it wasn't. I'd been talked into this job over the phone. They of course knew me well enough and I was pretty sure that there hadn't been any other candidates anyway, but it had never occurred to me to ask if they had changed grounds or anything. I had just told the Chairman to get the players together for a first training session so that I could start to get to know them, and I had said that I would meet him at the ground. No doubt he assumed that, being a local boy, I knew where the ground was, but I hadn't been home for over twenty years and I hadn't thought that the club could ever have moved. Still, that wasn't a bad thing. The new ground had to have better facilities than the old one, and a better playing surface too for that matter. As soon as the first rains of winter had come the pitch had turned back into the marsh it had always been and the players had had to scramble like pigs through the mud. I remembered that all right, how you'd start to dribble the ball and it would get left behind, stuck fast in the mud. Fortunately, then, I had been a fullback, and the little grass that remained on the pitch had been on the wings, and so I had still been able to use my pace to get past opponents and get in some good crosses.

We had been a funny mixture of a group back then, ex-cons from the island's prisons, a few of the guards too, steelworkers from the factory by the railway line, petty thieves who hadn't been caught yet, but who you knew wouldn't last the season, shop workers and mechanics, a barman, and, of course, me, a sixteen year old grammar school kid with the appearance of a bundle of sticks tied loosely together around the waist.

I remember the first time I had turned up at the ground with my little map and my small kit bag and I had pushed through those big red gates and somehow managed to force my shaking legs to carry me towards the changing rooms. At the entrance to the changing rooms standing by the pitch were two older men in tracksuits.

"What d'you want sonny?" one of them asked me roughly. I swallowed hard, my throat so dry it was painful, and tried to answer. But I was so scared that I couldn't get any words out.

"Well, what is it?" said the other man obviously irritated that I had interrupted their conversation.

"I know," laughed the first one, "you're 'ere for a trial, ain't ya son?"
I nodded weakly.
"It's Bill's boy," he told the other man.
"Bill? Bill who for fuck's sake?"
"Bill who plays cricket wiv us at Minster."

"Oh, that Bill. Didn't know 'e 'ad any kids. Didn't even know 'e was married."

"'Is wife ran off years ago and left 'im wiv a kid. What's your name sonny?"

I tried my hardest to answer, I really did, but nothing happened.

"Who gives a fuck what 'is name is," snorted the other man, "he don't look like a footballer for god's sake does 'e?"

"Bill talked about 'ow good 'e was all summer. Pestered me to death about giving 'im a trial for the reserves now that 'e's sixteen, if I'd 'ave seen 'im before I'd 'ave said no, f'sure, but 'e's 'ere now. Might as well let 'im train wiv us tonight."

"Whatever. Your time you're wasting."

"Come on Billy Boy, I'll take you inside," and he placed an arm around my shoulders and led me down the tunnel, and I never did tell him my name and he never asked again, and I became Billy from then on.

The changing room was small and cramped and overpowering and I felt sick at once. From that day on, the smell of horse liniment, deep heat, male sweat and foot odour were to become so much a part of my life that I grew used to it, but that first experience left a long-lasting impression. I wriggled into a corner and placed my kit bag on the wooden bench, trying to breathe only through my mouth. I took out my football boots, and their familiar damp feel helped me to relax just a little.

"Won't be needing them mate," said the large tattooed man beside me. I looked up at him. "We'll be runnin', not playin'. Keep your trainers on, it's concrete all the way to the beach."

I took his advice and kept my trainers on and then followed the others as they left the changing room as if by some pre-arranged signal. The man had been right, we didn't even touch the grass of the pitch, instead we filed out of the main gates and set off at a fast jog, following the Reserve Team Manager, who had been the one who had taken me to the changing rooms.

Someone coughed loudly close by, snapping me back to the present. An old man stood there bent over a walking stick.

"You looking for someone young man?"

"I was looking for the football ground," I told him.

"Football ground? The United ground?"

"Yeah, the United ground. It used to be 'ere didn't it?"

"Used to be, sure," said the old man. "They bulldozed it ten years ago now for these 'ouses. When were you 'ere last?"

"Last time I came 'ere was nearly twenty-three years ago."

"That explains it. Why 'ave you come looking for Sheppey United after so long?"

"I'm the new Manager," I told him, feeling decidedly foolish at my situation.

"You ain't …," he stammered.

"Yes, I am," I told him.

"Christ Almighty, I 'eard about it on the radio. I didn't think it were true."

"It's true," I assured him.

"Christ Almighty. Wait 'til I tell my missus I've met you. I saw you play once, when you was a kid. You was too good for United."

"You gotta start somewhere," I told him.

"Sure," he agreed nodding slowly.

"So, where's the new ground?" I asked realising that if I didn't get a move on I was going to be late for my first training session as a manager, and that wasn't a good example to set to my team. I imagined that the new ground would be on the outskirts of town. A compact little place with a nice playing surface and a tiny plastic stand, and a big car park for Sunday morning car boot sales which were without doubt the club's best income.

"What new ground?" asked the old man.

"Well, if they don't play 'ere anymore, they must play somewhere..."

"They play in Fav'sham."

"Faversham?"

"Yeah, Fav'sham. They play their matches at Fav'sham Town."

"Shit, I ain't never gonna get to Faversham in time for training."

"If it's only training then you'll find 'em at the ground by the steelworks."

"The Sheerness Steel Ground?"

"You know it?"

"Sure, you can see it from the train."

10

"Yes, that's it. Go straight on, take the first right, that's the quickest way."

"Thanks very much. I hope you'll come see us play."

"Don't think so, not in Fav'sham."

"I understand."

"But if the team comes back to the island, well, maybe."

I shook hands with the old man and hurried off to find the training ground, relieved that at least I didn't have to get to Faversham. The Sheerness Steel Ground was still set up for cricket with the square roped off to keep the kids from it. There were no goals in sight, and no players either, although I knew it was still early. I had arranged to meet the club chairman before training, to chat over a few things. I saw a lone BMW parked up near the gates to the ground and I hurried over to it. Seeing me coming the elderly man inside got out to meet me.

"Well, well, well, Billy Steed," he gushed taking my hand and pumping it enthusiastically, "Who'd 'ave thought that an ex-England captain'd come and manage our little club."

"Pleased to meet you Mr. Chairman."

"Please, call me Bob," he said, still holding my hand as if he were afraid that I would run away.

"I went to the old ground," I told him.

"What? The Botany Road Ground?"

"Yeah, I didn't know it 'ad been pulled down. I ain't bin 'ere since the last game I played back in 1985."

"It was sold to pay off debts. 1985 huh, those were the Southern League days, the club's greatest moments. And you were the club's greatest player."

"Well, I dunno. So we play our home games at Fav'sham Town."

"At the moment yes, but there might be a few problems with that for this season."

"What d'you mean?"

"We owe Faversham several thousand pounds in back rent. They won't let us play there until we clear the debt. They're a small team too. They need the money."

"So what's gonna happen?"

The Chairman gave a tired shrug.

11

"I dunno. I was thinking 'bout winding the club up. No ground, no fans and no manager, and then you called out of the blue and I got all enthusiastic again. Keeping this team going's costing me a fortune though."

"So there's no money left from the sale of the ground?"

"No, not a penny."

"So there ain't never gonna be a new ground then."

"No. Never."

"Shit."

"Listen, I understand if you want to walk away, I didn't realise you weren't aware of the situation. You should manage a league club."

"No one'd 'ave me," I told him, "I've spent the six months since I got out applying for every football job that's come up. Most clubs didn't even bother to call back. I couldn't even get an interview to be a tea boy. So that's when I thought I should go back to my roots and start again. I didn't know there wasn't already a manager 'ere. I thought I could 'elp with training, maybe you know, with the youth team or the reserves."

"We don't 'ave a youth team and we don't 'ave a reserve team."

"No, I guessed that. So, we might not even be able to start the season then?"

"If you're gonna stick around I'll see what I can do. Maybe we'll give this club just one more year. Who knows, with you 'ere we might even win a match."

"We didn't win a single match last season?"

"No. We drew a few. But we was relegated before Easter."

"Relegated? So what division are we in now? I didn't know you could get relegated from Kent League One. I thought Division Two was for reserves."

"It's all changed. There's the Kent League Premier Division now, where we were last year, and now we're in Division One (East)."

"It's a long way from the Southern League," I sighed. I hadn't envisaged my starting from the bottom being quite so far down, but I'd made a commitment and I wasn't a quitter, and besides when I'd said no one else wanted me I'd been telling the truth. I'd rung all my old clubs and begged for a position and been refused. I tried Sheppey United in last gasp desperation, without realising that they were in as bad a state as

I was. If truth be told we probably needed each other or maybe even deserved each other. This was the club that had given me a start and I wanted to give something back.

"So what d'you say? Are you up for it?"

"I'm staying," I said. I couldn't think of anything I could do with my life that wasn't connected with football, and this was the only job football was going to offer me. I'd started at the bottom once before, so I could start there again and this time I didn't have anything to lose.

A group of five young lads approached from the direction of the housing estate, kit bags over their shoulders and I realised that they were the first of my team. It was good to see them, I'd had a nagging doubt at the back of my mind that no one would turn up, that no one would want to play in a team managed by me. An old banger approached down the road at breakneck speed and skidded to a stop in front of the gates, just missing the Chairman's silver BMW but spraying it with gravel nonetheless.

"Bloody hell Ginger, you little yobbo," shouted Bob, the Chairman, shaking his fist at the driver of the wreck that had just arrived. The driver just laughed and he and his mates climbed out.

"That got you worried didn't it Bob," laughed the boy.

"What worries me is that I know you don't 'ave insurance."

"You can't get insurance for a car what's bin chored," one of the other lads informed him matter-of-factly.

"You could at least steal something better next time," said the Chairman.

"The beauty of choring an old wreck is that no one cares," laughed Ginger. "Although I might wanna upgrade to a BMW someday soon."

"You'll end up in the nick son," stated the Chairman. Then he looked at me as if to say he wished he hadn't mentioned prison, but I knew I would have to get used to worse than that and I pretended I wasn't bothered. Another car pulled up, almost as scruffy as Ginger's with panels of different colours and a broken window covered with cardboard.

The new lads approached until they stood together with the others in a small group around us.

"This, lads, as I'm sure you all know, is Billy Steed," began the Chairman, "Gillingham, Queens Park Rangers, Arsenal and England, and, of course, Sheppey United. You're new manager, listen carefully to what 'e says 'e 'as a lot to teach you."

"'E can teach Ginger 'bout life inside," whispered someone, and that got a good laugh.

"'E'll be right at 'ome with Charlie Chalk," added someone else and that got another round of laughter, although I didn't know who Charlie Chalk was.

"Thanks Mr. Chairman. Great to meet you lads," I said when the laughter had died down. "Our Club is in a terrible situation but the Chairman has agreed to give us financial support for this season, so we'll work hard and make sure he isn't wasting his money. My target for this season is promotion back to the Premier Division." Someone stifled a laugh. "Nothing else is good enough. The push for promotion starts right here today, right now." I paused for a moment to let my words sink in and then I counted the lads before me, the five who had walked from the housing estate and then the two carloads of four, we had thirteen players. "Is this everyone Mr. Chairman?" I asked.

"Everyone but Charlie Chalk," said Ginger.

"Where's he then?" I asked.

"Still back at 'is 'otel I guess," laughed Ginger and the others joined in.

"He's in the Open Prison at Eastchurch," said the Chairman, "he's allowed out to play matches, but not for training."

"'E's our star striker," put in Ginger, obviously the mouthy one of the team. "'E's been our top scorer for the last three seasons."

"Oh, really? We 'ave a star striker? That's good news. 'Ow many goals did 'e get last year? Not many I guess as we didn't win a single game."

"Seven," mumbled Ginger.

"Seven? Our star striker got seven?"

"He weren't allowed out for three months 'cause 'e got drunk after one of the matches," put in the Chairman.

"We're gonna need more than seven goals from 'im if we're gonna get promotion," I said.

"I was second top scorer," put in Ginger helpfully.

"Really? How many did y'get?" I wanted to know. "Five.?"

"Nah, three."

"You're forgettin' 'bout Big Jim," laughed someone, "'e got four."

"Own goals don't count mate," retorted Ginger.

"Who's Big Jim?" I asked.

"'E pissed off halfway through the season, said 'e were fed up wiv lettin' in s'many goals."

"'E was our keeper?"

"Yeah, worst 'keeper a team ever 'ad," said Ginger.

"Who's the keeper now?" I asked looking around expectantly at the group.

"We ain't got one. My cuz did it, but he said he couldn't be arsed this year."

"Well, you'd better tell 'im to come back, we ain't gonna get far without a keeper."

"Don't worry Boss, we'll make 'im, we'll break 'is arms or somethin'."

"I don't think a keeper with broken arms is gonna be any use, do you?"

"Nah, I guess not. We'll just kneecap 'im then, if necessary."

"Okay, why don't you all go and get changed and we'll get started." The group made a reluctant move towards the changing rooms, but the Chairman called them back.

"Uh, sorry lads we don't 'ave the keys for the changing rooms. we're not supposed to train here during the cricket season, the groundsman opened the gates as a special favour." With a groan the players dropped their kitbags to the floor and began stripping off their tracksuits.

"Where's the footballs?" I asked the Chairman, expecting him to produce a load from the huge boot of his BMW.

"I don't know. Ginger, who normally brings the footballs?" he called out.

"I've got one in the back of me car. Didn't think we'd be using a ball. Thought it would be just runnin'."

"Don't worry, while I'm in charge we'll always use a ball."

"Great," called Ginger as he dashed across towards his car to get the ball.

I'd always hated pre-season training as a player, actually, any training for that matter. The press always talk about so-and-so being a model professional for the way he spends hours doing extra training whilst the other players are in the pub, but they never said that about me at any stage in my career, indeed, I was always the first one in the pub.

I'd almost quit Sheppey United after my first training session. The Reserve Team Manager had taken us off on a jog that went further than I had ever walked in my life. From the ground, we ran alongside the railway track back towards the station, crossed the main road and headed up towards the beach. When we reached the beach we set off across the pebbles towards Minster, leaping the groynes and splashing through the rock pools. It soon became apparent who were the members of the first team as they bounded easily along at the shoulder of the leader, whilst the reserves straggled along behind, coughing and blowing and concentrating hard on not puking. I found my natural position at the back of the pack alongside the big tattooed man from the corner of the changing room who was so far the only player I knew.

"Jesus fuckin' Christ," he wheezed, "goalkeepers shouldn't 'ave to do this shit." I couldn't reply because I needed every ounce of oxygen in my lungs in order to keep running, but I nodded at him in understanding. Defenders shouldn't have to do it either I thought. We reached the seafront at Minster and headed inland back towards the main road. We came out by the cricket ground where my dad played and I realised just how far we'd come from Sheerness, and just how far we had to go to get back. I was sure I wouldn't make it, I was sure the big goalkeeper at my side wouldn't make it either. It wasn't long before we were left behind on our own, but we plodded doggedly on together, heads bowed, hearts pounding and muscles screaming. Eventually my companion ground to a halt and slumped forward, hands on knees, gasping for air. He stayed that way for a few minutes until he had regained enough strength to straighten up a bit.

"Go on without me mate," he gasped seeing me there at his side.

"Don't worry, I'll stay," I told him.

"They'll think you couldn't 'ack the pace," he wheezed, "you wanna create a good impression it's your first day."

"It's okay, when they give me a ball they'll see what I can do." We set off walking back in the direction of the football ground, both panting like heat-crazed dogs, the goalkeeper's face bright purple and fit to burst. I wasn't walking with him out of compassion, simply because I was glad to have stopped running and because I didn't know how to get back on my own, my dad hadn't thought to draw me a map of the whole damn island.

When the football ground eventually came into view, we started a slow jog up to the gates, not that we fooled anyone. Inside the ground the players were doing doggies, team relays back and forth between cones that had been placed on the pitch.

"We thought you'd got lost mate," laughed the First Team Manager to the big goalkeeper as we walked past. The doggies session finished a couple of minutes later and at last everyone returned to the changing rooms for boots and shin pads and from somewhere a ball was produced and some yellow training bibs. If I had thought that I was at last going to get a kick of a ball I was wrong. The First Team Manager called his players over and began to hand out bibs to the eleven he wanted to start, whilst the rest of us grouped around the Reserve Team Manager and awaited selection. Not surprisingly, I wasn't chosen to start, and I stood on the sidelines with the other non-starters. A one-sided game began with the yellow bibs giving our lot the run around, I watched them, so arrogant, so confident in their own ability and I longed to be one of them. At that moment in my life the only thing I aspired to was to be given a yellow bib.

There were no bibs at Sheppey United now, but at least we had a football, even if it was mostly bald and had probably been in the back of Ginger's car when he had stolen it. I squeezed it and found it predictably a bit flat, but it was all we had. As a token gesture towards fitness training I took the group on a lap of the sports field. As we came round to complete the lap I realised that they were expecting more and so we did a second and then a third, but I didn't think they could manage a fourth and I let them collapse, gasping, to the ground to recover. After a few minutes I got them back on their feet and divided them into two groups of six. I kept Ginger apart. I then picked up four kitbags and formed a large square. I got six of them to take their shirts off so we could tell who was against who, and I got them playing two-touch keep ball. I stood next to Ginger and asked him to call out the names of the players each time they touched the ball, so that I would get to know them.

"So, tell me, why do they call you Ginger?" I asked him one time when the ball had disappeared out towards the fence, "I mean, you haven't got red hair."

"'Ave you seen me legs?" he asked with a laugh. I looked down and realised that his legs were as thin as my arms. "Everyone thinks that when I tackle someone one of me legs is gonna snap, so Ginger Snap. Ginger for short." I pulled off one of the other players to talk to and put Ginger on in his place. I did that with all of them, getting to know them a little, asking them where they played or where they'd like to play.

The Reserve Team Manager of the 1984/85 season had left me until last, and I guessed that the session must be reaching an end when he finally asked my where I normally played.

"Fullback," I mumbled.

"Fullback? Left or right?"

"Either."

"Either?"

"I can kick with both feet," I told him. And I could, my dad had made me kick with both feet from the day I could walk and had spent hours with me over the park endlessly kicking a ball back and forth from one to the other. Other kids rode bikes or played soldiers or watched TV, I just played football with my dad. He'd had a trial for Fulham once, or so he said. It was hard to imagine really.

Next time the ball went out of play I was put on at left back. I know he chose left back because the First team right winger had been giving our defender the run around, and the best way to discard me was to have me made to look stupid as quickly as possible. It took a few minutes for the ball to get over to our side, but when it did the winger pushed the ball past me and set off after it, just as he'd been doing to the other fullback for the last half an hour. This time he didn't get anywhere near it, I turned chased after the ball and pushed it back to our keeper who cleared it long up field. The next time he got the ball he tried exactly the same thing, and once again I outpaced him with ease, this time I took a few seconds on the ball and cleared it up the touchline myself. The final whistle blew and we returned to the changing rooms. We could hear buoyant laughter from the First Team in the Home Changing Room, but our room was quiet save for the rasping breathing of the smokers as they struggled to light a first cigarette.

"Okay lads, not bad," said the Reserve Team Manager when he came in. "It'll get easier from now on, the first session is always the 'ardest. See you on Thursday and we'll do it all again." There was a collective groan and he went out again before we started to throw things at him. I took my time changing as I didn't want to be the first to leave, and besides I hoped that the Manager would come back in and tell me if I should return on Thursday with the others or not. He didn't come back, and so I made to leave.

"See you on Thursday kid," said the big goalkeeper, "that's some pace you've got there."

"Bye mate," I said.

I walked out of the changing rooms and headed for the gates. I was half way through when I heard someone calling out to me.

"Hey Billy Boy, 'old on a second," it was the Reserve Team Manager. "Make sure you come back on Thursday, I'll give you longer next time. If you're really as quick as you looked tonight maybe we could use you after all, though you don't look like a footballer. Tell your dad I said hi and tell 'im to feed you up a bit, you ain't nothin' but skin and bone."

I set off back towards the train station as night closed in around me. I was still feeling sick from the run that we had done and every muscle in my body hurt like hell, but at least they had noticed me, and deep inside I felt happier than ever before in my life.

TWO

The next morning I had a quick breakfast at my hotel and then I was back on the train over to the island. The Chairman met me at the station and we drove out from Sheerness heading for the prison at Eastchurch. The plan was to talk to the Governor to try to get him to allow Charlie Chalk to attend training sessions as well as matches, although the Chairman didn't think there was much hope of his agreeing. Apparently the previous Manager had asked as well and been refused. But the previous manager hadn't been Billy Steed had he.

As we approached the prison I was surprised to find that I had begun to sweat and that my heart was beating faster than usual. I guess seven years inside would do that to you. We got signed in by security and I heard the terrible and all too familiar clang as the gates closed behind us. A guard escorted us towards the main buildings and the governor's office. On the way, we skirted a beautiful football pitch. Its lush green surface looked as if it had been prepared as a bowling green rather than a football pitch, and it was big too. I'd always liked to play on a big pitch, it gave me room to use my pace to get away from opponents. Obviously the prison had a large team of groundsmen with nothing to do all day except sew mail bags and care for their grass. I could imagine a whole row of prisoners on hands and knees inspecting every blade and plucking out any that weren't a perfect shade of green.

The Governor was nice enough, understanding of our problem, but informed us that it was more than his job was worth to let Charlie Chalk out for training as well as matches.

"Charlie's got a parole hearing in December. He could be out by Christmas. You'll just have to wait 'til then."

"What about if we come 'ere to train?" I suggested.

"What d'you mean?" asked the Chairman.

"Well, if Charlie ain't allowed out, then what about the rest of us coming 'ere? I mean, the facilities are superb, you've seen the pitch, what about it Mr. Governor?"

"I don't know."

20

"What about if we agree to play a couple of friendlies 'ere? One against the guards and one against the inmates. That'll provide the prisoners with some entertainment don't you think?"

"Sounds okay, when would you want to start?"

"'Ow about tomorrow, Thursday?"

"Tomorrow? All right. I suppose you'd like to see Charlie now that you've come all this way."

"You read my mind," I laughed.

A guard led us from the Governor's office to the visiting room and we met Charlie Chalk. He was a tall thin youth in his very early twenties with tattoos all the way up his long arms. He looked what he no doubt was, a bit of a thug and petty criminal. I had seen plenty of his sort during my time in prison. They were the ones who had come along to my football coaching sessions and showed a bit of talent, but when you put them in a match situation they would lose their heads at the first rough tackle and want to start throwing punches. It was going to be a tough job keeping this young man in line, he looked like a sending off just waiting to happen.

We left the prison and headed back along the main road through Minster, past the cricket ground and on towards Sheerness.

"We've got one more person to see this morning Bob, if that's al'right with you?"

"Who's that?"

"Do you know Clive's Coaches?"

"Sure, out at Halfway."

"Then that's where we need to go. We need to get some team transport and Clive's our man."

"The Club can't afford to 'ire coaches, we just don't have any money. I'm sorry but the players are expected to make their own way to games."

"And they don't get expenses, right?"

"No, they don't."

"Well, I don't think it's right to expect players to pay their own petrol. Besides, you've seen their cars, more than likely one Saturday afternoon we'll be a third of a team short at three o'clock with someone broken down on the hard shoulder somewhere."

"That's all well and good, but as I said we just don't have any money. There's no gate receipts or nothing, any money we spend comes directly out of my pocket."

"Don't worry, this ain't gonna cost you a penny."

"I don't understand."

We arrived at Clive's Coaches and found Clive underneath one of his vehicles doing some repairs. His secretary informed him who we were and he cleaned his oily hands on a rag before offering me one to shake.

"Well I never, Billy Steed, al'right mate?"

"Al'right Clive. You ain't changed a bit."

"Right," he snorted, "apart from losing all me 'air, ageing twenty years and puttin' on ten stone?"

"Yeah, apart from that."

"Let's go into my office and get some coffee. I assume you've come to talk football."

"Yeah, we've come to talk Sheppey United."

"I 'eard you'd bin appointed Manager on the radio. It was a bit of a shock."

"For you and me both mate."

We went into Clive's small office and his secretary brought in three tasteless coffees and a plate of tasteless digestives the ones without chocolate.

"So, what brings the famous Billy Steed back to Sheppey United after all these years?"

"No one else'd 'ave me," I told him honestly enough.

"That figures. must 'ave bin tough inside."

"You've no idea."

"So, what can I do for you?"

"I need an Assistant Manager. Someone who knows the Kent League scene. And I couldn't think of anyone better than you."

"Not sure we need an Assistant Manager do we?" interrupted the Chairman looking worried.

"Sure we do, and don't worry, Clive knows I ain't offering him a salary."

"You ain't?" asked Clive his face in false shock.

"There ain't no money Clive, the club is bankrupt, we don't even pay expenses, even I don't get expenses."

"So why do it?"

"Because this is where I started. If it weren't for Sheppey United I'd never 'ave been a professional. I can't just let the club disappear without a fight. You played for 'em too, much longer than I did, you know how I feel."

"I guess so, but I ain't gonna pay off the debt to Fav'sham if that's why you're 'ere. I 'eard about that on the radio an' all."

"No. I need an Assistant Manager, a physio at matches and a minibus driver. That's the complete job description."

"You got a minibus then?"

"Nah, course not," I laughed, "but you 'ave."

"Sure, I've got twenty-two of the fuckers, but what's in it for me?"

"Well, you get to be my Assistant Manager. You get to spend Saturday afternoons in the pouring rain watching Kent League football and you get your company name on our shirts as club sponsor."

"So, I give you free transport in return for my name on the shirts? Is that it?"

"Obviously you'll 'ave to pay for the kit too."

"Obviously."

"'Ome and Away strips."

"Obviously."

"And tracksuits."

"Tracksuits?"

"Yeah, you can't imagine the clothes these kids turned up in for training yesterday. If we want them to play as a team they've got to look like a team."

"We never 'ad tracksuits."

"Don't worry Clive there's gonna be a huge amount of publicity over the next few months. Trust me, I've got big plans for this club."

"Sounds like fun," he said after a moment's thought, "it'll get me out of goin' to the Savacentre with the missus on Saturdays. I'll talk to my boy and get 'im to play as well. 'E was wiv Sittin'bourne Reserves last year."

"Didn't know you 'ad a son."

"A lot can 'appen in twenty-two years mate," he said with a broad smile. I liked Clive, I always had done. Maybe he was the closest thing to a friend I'd ever had.

I caught the train back to Sittingbourne and the Chairman returned to his construction company, which, fortunately, he was in the process of handing over to his son, which meant he was now able to spend more time on his hobby – Sheppey United Football Club.

I walked from the station under the graffiti- decorated subway to the Forum Shopping Centre, and then out to the High Street. Things hadn't changed much here since I was a kid. Many of the shops were still the same, although I didn't recognise any of the people. A few did a double take of my face as I walked past, I was starting to get used to that again. They knew they'd seen my face somewhere, but they couldn't remember where. Hours later no doubt they would realise who they had seen and rush to tell everyone they knew. But, let's face it, Sittingbourne High Street was the last place on earth you'd expect to see an ex-celebrity. I reached the Red Lion pub and had a sandwich for lunch washed down with a couple of pints of lager. I knew I shouldn't start drinking again, but what the heck, it was a hot day and I was celebrating having got us somewhere to train and having sorted out team transport. Clive was just as I had remembered him, and I was looking forward to the two of us working together. He shared my footballing philosophy. He and I had always gone against the Sheppey Manager's instructions about getting stuck in and hitting the ball long. Clive and I had always gone for the short passes and subtle touches, and the Manager had screamed at us until he was fit to burst, but we only knew how to play one way. Clive was five years older than me, but he had broken into the First Team that season when I started, and he sort of took me under his wing a bit and looked after me on and off the field. When I'd been signed by Gillingham I'd tried to get them to take him on too, but the scout they sent to watch him wasn't impressed, and so Clive spent his career at United and eventually took over his father's coach company, whilst I went on to other things and other places. I'd seen the whole world through football, Clive had rarely been out of Kent. I wondered who'd had the happier life of the two.

When I'd finished my lunch I set off down the High Street towards the offices of the local newspaper. The editor had asked to do a piece about my return to Sheppey United. I hated the press after what they'd done to me over the years, but I knew that my team needed all the publicity it could get.

The interview went okay. The editor said she didn't know too much about football and so her sports writer had asked the questions, except that at the end she had wanted to know how I planned to rebuild my personal life.

"My personal life is in just as bad a state as my professional life, as you can no doubt imagine. To be 'onest, I 'aven't given much thought to anything other than football since getting out of prison. Sheppey United has my full and undivided attention."

"That's it then," decided the Editor with a smile and she stood up to signal that I should leave. We shook hands and then I shook hands with the sports reporter.

"We went to the same school," he told me.

"Did we?"

"Yeah, Borden Grammar, you were a couple of years older than me, but I always followed your career, I think the whole town did."

"I guess I let a lot of people down."

"I guess you turned out to be just 'uman rather than some sort of superman."

"I thought I was Superman once. It's amazing 'ow quickly your life can change. It's amazing 'ow quickly you can lose everythin'."

"Well, it's never too late to put things right mate."

"I hope so."

"I'll try to find a picture of you and Clive from your playing days together for the story. I'm sure there must be a few in the archives. We gave a lot of coverage to Sheppey when they were in the Southern League."

"Great, it'll be nice to see Clive with hair again, I'm sure he'll appreciate it."

"Okay, well, we'll keep in touch. I'll try to cover a few of your home games this season."

"Great, see you soon then mate."

I walked back up the High Street and then turned into Central Avenue to find the library. I needed something to read in the evenings or I was going to fall into the terrible habit of going down to the hotel bar and drinking my life away. It's amazing just how many books you can get through in a seven year prison stint if you put your mind to it, so I wasn't too confident about finding anything new I wanted to read, but I'd have a good look. I went through the fiction section which was arranged alphabetically, but nothing caught my eye and I ended up at the back of the library with just the biography section to go. It was then that I heard a voice that I knew coming from behind another row of books about travel. I couldn't see the person the voice belonged to, but my heart had begun to beat faster and had obviously realised who it was before my brain had worked it out. It had been over twenty years since I had last heard that voice, but there was no mistaking it. I froze to the spot and sweat broke out all over my body all at once.

I listened to what the voice was saying trying to decide whether I should reveal myself or stay hidden and let the person go away.

"Look, I dunno which is best, I dunno nothin' about America, 'ow could I? I ain't never bin nowhere 'ave I."

I took a deep breath and walked around the row of books to see a woman and a boy of about eight.

"Maybe I can be of 'elp," I offered, "I've bin to America a few times."

The woman looked round at me instantly, no doubt she knew my voice just as I'd known her's. Her face drained of all its colour as if she had seen a ghost. Her hand reached up and clasped at her chest and she gasped for air.

"Oh my god!" she exclaimed, "it's you."

"Yeah, it's me. 'Ow's things?"

"'Ow's things?"

"Yeah, ow's things? I mean what've you bin up to for the last twen'y years?"

"Is it really twen'y years?"

"At least twen'y years."

"Christ, seems like yesterday."

"You ain't changed a bit," I told her, "you still look nineteen."

"Stop it," she said trying to hide her face with her hand so that I couldn't see her, "I don't look nineteen at all. Not after four kids."

"You've got four kids?"

"Yeah. Four kids. I've bin married three times."

"Three times? 'Ow d'you manage that?"

"I guess I ain't 'ad a lot of luck with men."

"I guess not."

It's extremely difficult to know what to say when you meet someone by chance after such a long time, someone you never thought you'd see again, someone who once meant so much. It's even harder when her young son is there, impatient to get the books he needs for his summer holiday project which he should have started weeks ago. I looked at her, she looked at me. The funny thing was, that for all the thousands of times I'd dreamed of meeting her again, I'd never bothered to prepare anything worthwhile to say.

"Well, I'd better be off," she said as her son tugged at her sleeve.

"Sure, nice to see you again."

"Listen, maybe, oh I dunno."

"What?"

"Maybe we could 'ave a coffee or somethin', y'know when I've got no kids around. I'll get my mum to look after 'em for a few 'ours."

"If you're sure that's all right."

"We can 'ave a coffee and a bit of a chat after all this time, can't we?"

"Sure."

"Where d'you live?"

"At the 'otel up on the 'ill."

"The Conistan?"

"Yeah, that's the one."

"Are you free Friday mornin', say eleven?"

"Sure, I don't 'ave anythin' to do these days."

"Okay, I'll come to your 'otel. Why d'you live in a 'otel?"

"That's what footballers do," I told her.

"You're a footballer?" asked the boy with a slight hint of interest in his voice.

"You like football?" I asked him.

"Love it!"

27

"Who d'you support?"

"Ars'nal."

"Really? I used to play for them."

"You're joking."

"No, I was captain."

"You really played for Ars'nal?"

"And 'e was captain of England," put in the boy's mother.

"No way! Wait 'til I tell granddad. What's your name mister?"

"That's enough," said his mother, "it's time to go. You've got a project to do, remember?"

"See you Friday," I told her and I watched her hurry away and waited for my heart beat to return to normal. I went back to the biography section and found a book about Bill Shankly and also Brian Clough's autobiography. If I was going to be a football manager then where better to look for guidance than with two of the greatest?

Thursday evening I took the train over to the Island again. This time Clive was waiting for me in a minibus outside the station. We drove round to the training pitch and waited for the players to arrive and then hurried them into the bus for the drive to the prison. To say they were shocked to find that we had club transport was an understatement. Clive had persuaded his son to come along as he had said he would, but the boy, who was the spitting image of his father from twenty years before, was not sure that Sheppey United was the right move for him. Sittingbourne had a lot better prospects than their island rivals, that was obvious to anyone, but as his father rightly told him, Sittingbourne didn't have Billy Steed as Manager.

We reached the prison and were shown inside by a guard, and the team piled into the spotless changing rooms to prepare themselves for the session. Our star striker, Charlie Chalk, soon came to join us.

"Bet you feel right at 'ome 'ere Boss?" quipped Ginger.

"What 'appened to our goalie?" I asked ignoring his comment.

"'E said, and I quote, "tell Billy Steed to go fuck 'isself,'" so I guess he ain't comin'."

"Let's make that the last time you swear in my dressing room, okay Ginger?"

"Wot? You can't get sent to prison for swearing can ya? Don't tell me you got ten years for swearing Boss?"

"Come on everyone, let's hurry up and get outside," I shouted and left the changing room. Clive was out on the pitch juggling the new football I had bought that afternoon. Seeing me walking onto the pitch he kicked it over to me. I controlled it instantly, without thinking, and flicked it casually back to him.

"Brings back some memories hey mate?" laughed Clive.

"Yeah, sure does mate," I agreed.

"Remember that goal I scored down at Dover in the fog one time, we did one-twos all the way up the pitch and no one could touch us."

"Sure I remember," I lied. I'd scored a goal in an FA Cup Final at Wembley, taken and missed a penalty in the Nou Camp and been sent off in the San Siro, how was I supposed to remember a fucking foggy game down in Dover for Christ's sake? Those were the kind of games that you tried to forget.

"Best goal I ever scored," continued Clive to himself. "What was the best goal you ever scored mate? That one for England 'gainst Scotland was a cracker d'you remember that one?"

"Sure I remember, it was meant to be a cross but the wind blew it over the keeper and into the top corner."

"Rubbish, you meant that all the way. You picked up the ball, looked up, saw the keeper off his line and delicately chipped it over 'im."

"There was a gale force wind blowing Clive, no one could have done a delicate chip over the keeper in those conditions. I just got lucky, my first game as captain too, the perfect start."

"Is it your ambition to manage England one day?"

"Fuck off! England don't 'ave ex-cons as managers for Christ's sake!"

"There's a first time for everythin'."

"Right now, let's concentrate on not getting Sheppey United relegated this year, that's our top priority."

"Relegated? You mean we ain't playing for promotion?"

"Sure we're playing for promotion, at least to begin with, but I don't think it's gonna be easy – you ain't seen our lads play yet."

"And you ain't seen the opposition they're up against. This ain't the Second Division y'know, or even the poxy Southern League. No, for fuck's sake, this is the Kent League Division One fuckin' East, this is almost as low as you can get mate."

"Well, let's not get relegated to Division Two fucking East then, that's all I'm saying."

"We'll be al'right, don't worry. You've got enough experience to get this lot playin' as a good team. You played under some of the best managers in the game, somethin' must've rubbed off on you."

"Let's 'ope so." The players started to emerge from the changing rooms, tumbling out like sweets from a packet of liquorice allsorts. Time to get them together for a chat about my footballing philosophy and how we were going to try to play things over the next few months.

It was a balmy late summer evening and I sat the players down on the beautiful grass. They were all so young that they probably couldn't remember seeing me play on TV, so they might not be aware of how I had played the game myself.

"The game's called football," I began, "and that's what we're gonna do, play football. Always. It's about winning. It's all about winning. As long as I'm manager 'ere we'll try to win every game, no matter who we're playing against. I promise you I'll never say 'we're playing for a draw 'ere today or a point away from 'ome is good,' that ain't my way. If it's one-all with ten minutes to go and we're away from 'ome then we're still gonna try and win." I paused to let my words sink in a bit. No one spoke, everyone was looking down at the grass.

"Football's about possession. If you ain't got the ball you have to get it back as quickly as possible, and once you've got it you need to keep it. The more you 'ave the ball, the more chances you can create and chances mean goals. You might think as a former defender I might wanna teach you that good defence is the key to victory, but it ain't. I was a defender, but I was always looking to put my team onto the attack. Right Clive?"

"Right Boss," responded Clive quietly.

"I've played for some of the best defensive managers in the business, guys who 'ad teams of people checking out the opposition to find their strengths and then come up with ways of stopping 'em from playing. We ain't gonna do that. Let the opposition worry 'bout us. We're only gonna play one way. Always." Ginger raised his head to look at me as if he wanted to speak.

"What's up Ginger?"

"So, Boss, we don't just knock the ball long to Charlie Chalk no more?"

"'Ow many games did you win last season doing that?" I asked although of course I already knew the answer.

"None."

"So that obviously didn't work, did it?"

"Guess not."

"It's all about dominating possession, and you do that in midfield. We'll be playing five in midfield against everyone else's four, and that extra man will give us more possession."

"So, just me up front then?" asked Charlie Chalk.

"No, we play two up front, otherwise we ain't gonna score enough goals."

"You mean we're gonna play three in defence?" put in Clive.

"Yeah."

"What? Two full backs and just one centre back?" he wanted to know.

"No. We won't 'ave full backs. We're gonna play with two centre backs and a sweeper. Most teams play with two up front, you don't need four people to mark two, it's a waste."

"Sounds suicidal to me," said Ginger.

"Not if we keep possession. All the time we've got the ball the other team can't attack us, can they? That's what Clive and I are gonna teach you over the next few weeks – 'ow to keep the ball. Okay, let's get started." I got to my feet and headed for the centre of the pitch.

We played for nearly two hours, always two-touch, in a large grid marked out with tracksuit tops. We didn't do any fitness training, we just learned to move the ball around from one to the other. Clive and I played one on each side to make sure things were done the right way. As the sunlight began to fade and the shadows of the tall trees reached right across the pitch, we called it a day and set off back for Sheerness in the minibus. It was quiet on the way back, a peacefulness born out of hard work, and I was pleased with the way things had gone, considering it was only our second session together.

31

I stared out of the window of the minibus as we headed away from the prison and thought about my second training session with Sheppey United when I was a kid. I'd gone over to train on my own again, almost died on the run along the beach, just like the first time, walked back from Minster with the Second Team goalie and missed the doggies. Once more I was a substitute for the Reserves when the kick about match finally began at the end of the session. I kept looking at our Manager, hoping that he remembered his promise to give me a bit more time, and eventually he must have felt the weight of my stare because he called me over to him.

"Can you really play both sides." He asked.

"Yes, I can," I assured him. "Okay, right back tonight then. Try and push forward a bit and 'elp out in midfield."

I slotted myself in at right back as the Reserves tried to soak up the First Team's unrelenting pressure. I'd lost count of how many goals they'd already scored, but they were hungry for more. As I had no one to mark, I pushed forward into the gap ahead of me a bit and waited for the ball to come my way. Eventually, there was a loose pass by one of the First Team and the ball found its way into some space in front of me. I pounced on it in a flash and began to run with the ball at my feet. No one came towards me at first, they probably thought that I was so useless that I'd just trip over or something, and so I was over the half way line and bearing down on their penalty area before someone with a yellow bib came across to try to tackle me. I pushed the ball around him and sprinted away, skipped over a lunge from their left back, and then I was clean through on goal. The keeper rushed out to meet me, but I simply chipped the ball over his head and into the waiting goal beyond. There was a sort of stunned silence and then the First Team Coach, who had been refereeing, blew his whistle for the end of the game. As I approached the dressing room, the big goalkeeper who was my running partner caught up with me and slapped me on the back.

"Great goal kid. You shoulda seen the First Team Manager's face when that went in!" he laughed. Once inside, our manager enthused about how well we had played, although we all knew we had been shit, and he said we were improving in a lot of areas. I don't think anyone believed him. I said goodbye to the goalkeeper and went to leave.

"Nice goal Billy," called out the Manager, "you'll get to play from the start next time, really show us what you can do."

I hurried to the train station. I couldn't wait to get home to tell my father about my goal, it was as if I'd scored the winner in the FA Cup Final or something.

THREE

I spent a restless night going over in my mind the things I had seen at training, doubting the way we were going to play, wondering if my ideas could ever work. What if we lost every game? That would be the end of my managerial career and what would I do then? Also, I worried about having coffee with Christine. Fuck. I was so stupid. What was the point of seeing her again after all these years? What could we possibly have to say to each other? What could we possibly have in common? She was a mother and would probably want to talk about her kids and I was an ex-con and there was no way we were going to talk about my time in prison. And I knew she hated football.

And yet, funnily enough, the first time I'd seen her was at a football match. I'd been twelve. It was my first game for my secondary school team and I'd been put in at left back because no one else could kick with their left foot. The team captain's fifteen year old sister had come along to watch and had dragged along her best friend, Christine. The two girls arrived on bicycles about twenty minutes after the game started, since they went to a girl's school on the other side of town, and positioned themselves somewhere near the halfway line on the far side from me.

I noticed Christine immediately. It was impossible not to. She was, without doubt, the most beautiful thing I had ever seen in my life. I had never taken an interest in the giggling girls in my class, but this was different. This was an older woman and I was besotted in an instant. I knew she hadn't noticed me. She was sitting on her bike playing with her long dark hair, her back to the game, chatting with her friend, and of course she was way out of my league. But, for some reason, I felt from the very first time I laid eyes on her that she was destined to be mine.

For the second half, we changed ends and my heart started to pump violently as I walked across the grass after the team talk to her side of the pitch. Imagine my disappointment when the girls immediately took off for home, reluctant no doubt to endure another half of tray-of-marbles football. I don't remember anything else about my first ever proper game of football, except that in the final minute of the game I gave away the goal that lost us the match. I was distraught, not because of the result, simply because I assumed that my error would cost me my place in the side for the next game and I wouldn't be able to see the beautiful girl with the long dark hair again. One thing I knew for sure was that the captain of our team was going to become a very close friend of mine from that moment on.

I felt shattered in the morning. Perhaps the effort I'd put in at training in the kick-about but more than likely just as a result of a night spent worrying about seeing Christine again. I hated myself for being such an idiot where she was concerned. Does everyone have someone in their life who just turns them into a fool? And does that someone know what they do to you? Still, love isn't a choice. We don't choose who we love, or how deeply we fall in love, it just happens and it's beyond our control. It wasn't my fault that, in all the years we'd been apart, I'd never been able to get her out of my mind. Don't get me wrong, I'm not saying I never looked at another woman or anything, of course I did. I was rich and famous and some women obviously thought I was good-looking and of course I was single, and I had a series of short-lived relationships right up until I went into prison. I'd dated some of the most beautiful models on the catwalk and several minor TV celebrities too. The problem was, I always compared my feelings with how I'd felt about Christine, and no one ever came close. That was why I had never got married. I would have wanted the person I married to make me feel how Christine made me feel every time I saw her, I would have wanted my heart to ache every second that we were apart, just as it had ached for Christine all these years.

I dragged out breakfast for as long as I could. I took my Brian Clough autobiography down with me and read as I sipped a coffee and nibbled at some toast. It was only nine o'clock. I decided to head out for a jog to try to clear my head a bit. From the hotel up on top of the hill with its view down across the town I headed away from the main road and through the Australian Estate. Then, I crossed Borden Lane and ran down Homewood Avenue. It was a long road but mostly downhill, and at the end I turned left and then first right. I hadn't set off on my jog with any particular destination in mind, but I couldn't deny where my legs were taking me. I crossed the main road that led down to the High Street and saw the entrance to the park ahead of me. When I reached the gates I stopped and turned to look behind me at the little terraced house where I had grown up. The façade was still a shabby grey pebbledash as it always had been, but the front door was now red when it had always been blue. There were three For Sale signs hammered into the little rose bed that made up the front garden, as if the owner were desperate to sell but no one was interested. My parents had bought it when they got married and my father had been left to pay the mortgage alone when my mother abandoned us. When my father had finally drunk himself to death by the time I was eighteen, I sold the place without any remorse at all. And I'd never had a place to call home since. I'd lived in boarding houses, hotels and club flats all my life, except for my time at Her Majesty's pleasure of course, which was my longest-lasting address since I left home.

When I got tired of looking at the house, I set off into the park. I knew the next stop would be our bench. The bench where Christine and I had always met up. The first time I had talked to her she had been sitting on that bench, the one on the far side of the park by the spiked railings of the old Grammar School. I jogged slowly round on the cinder track, alone except for an old man walking an old dog. I called out a greeting as I ran past but was ignored.

I found that our bench was gone, destroyed by vandals, only the cement base remained with a broken piece of wood attached at one end by twisted, rusty bolts. How many times had we met up at this bench? Thousands probably. Almost every day for almost five years. She was always there first, always waiting for me no matter how early I tried to arrive. I don't know how she did it. My house was right next to the park whilst hers' was way across on the other side of town. Sometimes, I would enter the park and see that she wasn't there yet, and I would set off running as fast as I could right across the middle of the wet grass to try to get there before her, but she would always show up from the dead end road at the side of the Grammar School and breeze up to our bench on her bike and I would arrive breathless and defeated.

"Why d'you run?" she would ask.

"To spend more time with you," I would pant and then collapse into her welcoming arms before she'd had a chance to even get off her bike. The one and only time I had ever got there before her was the last time we had arranged to meet and of course I had got there first because she had had no intention of coming at all.

The second time I had seen Christine had been in the park. It was a sunny Saturday morning and as always I was playing football with my friends. I had invited the captain of our school football team to come along but I hadn't mentioned that he should tell his sister or her beautiful friend. But, we'd only been playing for ten minutes or so when I saw a dark-haired girl on a bicycle appear from the road beside the Grammar School. At that precise moment in the game I had been clean through on goal, but I had just stopped and stared and someone took the ball off me and ran away with it. I didn't care. The captain of the school team came over to me.

" What's up?" he asked. Then he followed my gaze and saw the girl.

"That's Christine," he said, and so I found out her name. "She was s'posed to meet my sister 'ere, but she's gone to the Savacentre with my parents. I'll go tell her."

"I'll tell her," I decided and pushed past him. Suddenly, I felt my heart thumping so hard I thought it might hammer a way out through my rib cage. I saw her cycle up to the bench, leave her bike at the side and sit on top of the bench with her feet up on the wooden seat. Her long dark hair was in a single plait that ran down her back and she was wearing a black leather jacket, despite the warm weather. I was so nervous that my throat went completely dry in the space of just a few seconds. What could I possibly say to her that wouldn't make me sound like a stupid kid? How did older people of her age speak? She was fifteen, what could she possibly see in me? And yet I felt compelled to make myself talk to her. I knew I didn't care what she thought of me or what she might say to me, even if she was cruel. I just had to speak to her.

She must have watched me walking across towards her, a little spindly child with fragile sticks for arms and legs, his hair too long because his father never had any spare money to take him for a haircut, and I always thought that she must have wanted to laugh at me then. Who was I to dare to approach her? She must have had the eyes of every teenage boy in the village on her wherever she went, and here was an ugly, frail, twelve year old kid walking over to talk to her.

My brain was in such a turmoil that I didn't realise I had reached the edge of the grass, and suddenly I found myself stumbling down onto the cement path. The studs of my football boots couldn't grip and I slipped and fell and landed on my knees. I heard her try to stifle a laugh. I longed for the ground to swallow me up. I could have just run back to my football match, but my friends would have laughed at me, and so I made the brave decision to pick myself up and tell her what I'd come to tell her. I got unsteadily to my feet, just a couple of yards from her and I was so overawed by her beauty that I couldn't speak. I just looked at her like a fool. No doubt my mouth was hanging open.

"You al'right?" she asked. I didn't say anything, I couldn't. "You've cut yourself," she informed me. I glanced down and saw that both my knees were bleeding. I swallowed nervously and forced myself to speak at last.

"I'm al'right," I managed, trying to make my puny kid's voice sound like that of a more mature fourteen or fifteen year old. There was an awkward silence before I finally remembered that I was there to tell her something. I realised that I didn't know the name of the girl she was supposed to meet.

"Your friend ain't coming," I said.

"Okay, thanks. We was gonna go on a bike ride," she informed me and she sounded a little disappointed.

"I'll go with you," I offered. My heart was suddenly pounding so loudly that I quickly had to close my mouth certain that she would hear it.

"Finish your game first," she said. And so I reluctantly turned away from her and went back to the match. Of course my mind was now on other things and the game drifted by without me. Every now and then I would dare to glance over at the girl sitting up on the back of the bench. I had expected her to disappear off somewhere rather than wait for me, but to my surprise she remained. And so the game dragged on until mid-morning, until at last my friends grew tired. They sat down in a group to chat and recover a bit before drifting home. I picked up my tracksuit top from the goalpost pile and said goodbye and headed off towards the girl. I could feel the weight of my friend's stares on me as they watched me walk away. No doubt they thought I had gone mad.

"Where's your bike?" she asked.

"At my house," I told her and pointed to the little terraced houses that ran alongside the park. "I'll go get it."

"Want me to come?" she offered.

"Sure." And she jumped down from the bench and grabbed her bike, and we set off down the side of the park, me walking on the grass so that I didn't fall over again in my studs and she on the path.

"You played good," she said as we walked.

"No, I didn't," I laughed.

"Yeah, you did. How many goals d'you score?"

I shrugged. I really hadn't been concentrating on the football at all.

"Dunno. Wasn't counting," I told her.

"Must 'ave bin five or six," she offered.

"Maybe."

"Saw you play at the school," she said.

"Did you?"

"Yeah, you were the best player by a mile."

"I dunno," I replied. I couldn't believe that she had actually noticed me. At the time I hadn't thought that she was watching the game at all. I was glad that she hadn't stayed until the end and seen me give away the decisive goal.

"Didn't you see me?" she asked.

"Yeah, course," I told her. Of course I had seen her. I was about to blurt out that I had thought she was the most beautiful creature on God's earth the second I had laid eyes on her, but I just managed to stop myself. Just.

We reached the park gates and I carefully tiptoed across the road to my house, not wanting to fall over in front of her again.

"Wanna come in?" I offered.

"Nah. I'll wait out here," she decided and she leant her bike against the gate post and sat down on the low stone wall.

"Won't be long," I promised, still worried that she was going to disappear.

"S'okay, no rush. Get your mum to 'ave a butcher's at your knees. They're still bleeding." She pointed at my knees. I looked down. They were still bleeding.

"Don't 'ave a mum," I told her, and then I hurried down the alley at the side of my house and in through the back door which was always open. I called out to my father, but it was after eleven and the local pub was already open and I hadn't expected him to be at home. He tried to stay sober during the week to help me get through the difficulties of my life, but at the weekends the temptation was too great and I hardly ever saw him. I slipped my permanently wet boots off and left them in the back porch and then I raced upstairs. I ran into my father's bedroom at the front of the house and looked out of the window to check that the girl was still there. To my utter amazement she was, still sitting on the wall, playing with the end of her long plait.

I ran for the bathroom, shedding my clothes as I went. I turned both taps on full and jumped into the bath even though the water was freezing. I ducked my head under a tap and then applied some shampoo, worked it into a lather for about five seconds and then ducked my head under again to rinse. Then I cleaned my knees, both at the same time, one under each tap, turned off the water and climbed out of the bath. I hadn't even bothered to put the plug in. I grabbed a towel and raced into my bedroom. Fortunately, I didn't have many clothes to choose from, so I just pulled on my jeans and the cleanest-looking T-shirt I could find. I tucked my trainers and socks under my arm and headed for the stairs. With a sudden flash of inspiration I dived back into my father's room, checked that the girl was still there, and then grabbed a bottle of aftershave which I tipped quickly over my head. I towelled my hair dry with one hand as I raced down the stairs, pulled on my socks and trainers in the back porch, chucked the towel back into the kitchen and then I was out of the door heading for the shed to get my bike.

I hoped she wouldn't laugh at my bike. My father had brought it home for me one day saying he had been given it by a bloke in the pub, but I kind of thought he'd borrowed it from someone's front garden. It was part blue and part red as if it were different bikes cobbled together, but it was mostly grey where the paint had been bashed off. It was going to be a sorry sight indeed next to Christine's beautiful purple bicycle which looked almost new.

I wheeled my bike down the alley to the street and was amazed and relieved to find her still sitting on the wall waiting for me.

"That were quick," she said.

"Where we goin'?" I asked.

"Follow me," she told me and then she was on her bike and setting off on our ride. We went back into the park and through the gate in the far corner and out onto Bell Road. We headed away from the town centre into Woodstock Road and soon we were out of the town and into the country. I wondered how far we would go, but she hadn't mentioned a destination and so I just followed dutifully behind her. We climbed up the hill into Tunstall, side by side, past the church and through the village. Once we had passed the school she took the lead again as the road levelled out and we headed for Bredgar. Maybe that was our destination, although I didn't care. At that moment I would have followed her anywhere.

At the bridge over the M2 Motorway, we stopped and looked down at the speeding traffic for a while, but the girl soon got bored and we were off once more. I noticed that the sky was beginning to darken now after the sunshine of earlier and my stomach was telling me it must be close to lunchtime, but I wasn't about to cut short our ride.

In Bredgar, we stopped at the pond and watched the ducks glide gracefully across the filthy water. It was then that we felt the first spots of rain.

"We'd better get back," she decided, "'sides, it's nearly lunchtime." I nodded in agreement and we turned our bikes around and set off for home. We had just reached Tunstall when the heavens opened. Christine pulled in at the side of the road under a tall chestnut tree near the church and I stopped alongside her. She took off her leather jacket and held it up over her head. This was the bottom of the hill where the famous Gray Lady of Tunstall had often been seen. She was a terrifying, ghostly figure that would walk up the hill and disappear into the grave yard by the church. I tried to act unconcerned, although I was all too aware that many of my friends had seen her. I tried to convince myself that she wouldn't appear during the day time, although with the storm clouds overhead it was pretty dark.

"Quick, get under 'ere or you're gonna get soaked," she told me. I moved my bike in close to hers and ducked under her jacket, helping to hold it up over our heads. And suddenly we were face to face. I noticed some drops of water on her cheeks and I saw she had a small scar at the bottom of her chin, but most of all I felt drawn in by her eyes. And we looked into each other's eyes. And there was the incessant drumming of the rain on her jacket, the smell of leather mixed with my dad's cheap aftershave, but most of all were her eyes.

I could have stayed there with her that way forever, but after a while the rain eased off and we had to go.

"Bring a jacket next time," she whispered as she put hers back on. Next time? Had she really said next time? I couldn't believe it. I was so happy I thought my heart would burst.

Once we got back into town, she slowed as we went down Bell Road and then stopped at the end of the street that led to the park. I pulled up alongside her.

"Got to get 'ome now," she told me.

"Okay," I said. She made to move off without me, but I put my hand on her arm to stop her. I didn't want her to go without knowing that I'd heard her say next time and I wanted her to agree to see me again. But, of course, I didn't know what to say.

"What?" she asked.

"I'm playing football at school again on Wednesday," I managed to say, which was really stupid but was the only thing that came into my head.

"I know," she said and she smiled. And I let go of her arm and I watched her cycle away down the road until she was out of sight past the cemetery gates heading towards her side of town.

I had to walk home, pushing my bike, since my legs had begun to tremble uncontrollably. Once inside the house, I climbed the stairs to my room and collapsed on my bed. I stayed there for the rest of the day and into the night. I didn't eat or drink or listen to music or anything. It wasn't until after midnight that I heard the back door crash open and knew my father was finally home, drunk as usual. I heard him stumbling around for a while and then it went quiet. I hauled myself off my bed and went and got my father's duvet from his room. I carried it downstairs. I found him, as I often did, crashed out on the sofa. I carefully pulled off his boots, lifted his heavy legs up onto the couch and covered him with the duvet. I went to the kitchen to shut the back door and then I went back to bed. In the darkness, unable to sleep, I tried to blot out the sound of my father's snores and concentrate on the very faint smell of leather that I could just about still imagine in the air around me. The only thing that worried me was that I might be dropped from the school football team. Still, we had training Monday after class and I would have to pull out all the stops to make sure I got selected. Imagine Christine coming to see me play and finding out I wasn't even in the team!

FOUR

Back at my hotel I took a shower. Fortunately, I still didn't have many clothes to choose from, so I just pulled on my jeans and the cleanest-looking T-shirt I could find. I realised I wasn't really prepared for a date as I didn't even have any aftershave. Still, to call it a date would probably be the wrong terminology. Christine had said she'd been married three times, but she hadn't said she'd been divorced three times, so maybe husband number three was still around. Maybe he wasn't. Maybe she lived with someone else, a future husband number four perhaps. Fuck. Why did Christine always do my head in? What did I really think was going to come out of this meeting? Did I think we'd just have a coffee and a chat and then never see each other again? Did I think that by talking to her I might be able, at long last, to fall out of love with her? Could I somehow break the spell she had put on me? Maybe that was what I hoped. Although I knew in my heart that that was impossible.

Or did I think that we'd have a coffee, talk about old times and fall in love all over again? Or was I just desperate for sex? Did I think we'd have a quick coffee and then race upstairs to my little attic home and fuck like when we were teenagers? I decided that I should put sex firmly out of my mind, that wasn't going to happen. The most likely outcome was probably the one that worried me the most. She would be her old amazing self and I would make a fool of myself by telling her that I still loved her, that I'd always loved her, and she'd laugh at me for being so stupid. I was beginning to feel like an insignificant kid again, just as I'd always felt around her.

At a quarter to eleven, I left my room and went downstairs, not to wait for her, but to go out to get a newspaper. There was a newsagent's at the bottom of the hill and I bought my favourite daily and also a copy of the local paper to see if they'd bothered to print my interview or not. I walked back up the hill and went into the bar to wait for Christine. The bar was empty after the morning breakfast rush, so I sat in a corner and drank an orange juice and quickly searched through the gazette. They had indeed found an old photo of Clive and I celebrating a goal together. God we looked so young, and of course we had been. It seemed like a lifetime ago now. I wondered how many goals we would get to celebrate this season. What if my team couldn't even manage to score a goal? What then?

I looked at the clock over the bar. Ten past eleven. At what time was I going to decide that Christine wasn't coming? Quarter past? Half past maybe? Should I give her an hour just in case she'd been held up in traffic on her way along the A2? I finished my orange juice in one go and got up to leave. Christine was many things, she was a very complicated person, don't get me wrong, I'd always liked that, but one thing she was not, was late. If she wasn't there at eleven, then I knew in my heart that she wasn't going to show. She had always known what was best and I had always trusted her judgement. Maybe husband number three had heard that I was back in town and told her not to see me under any circumstances, although Christine had never been the type of person you told what to do.

As I exited the bar and walked across the lobby towards the stairs, I heard the phone at reception ring. I paused, one foot on the bottom step.

"Mr. Steed, it's for you," called out the young receptionist who steadfastly refused to call me Billy. My heart started to beat a little faster. Thank god. It had to be her calling to say that she was still coming. Maybe her car wouldn't start or she'd had to pick up a prescription for one of her kids or something.

"Hello?" I answered.

"Hey mate, you seen our photo yet?" It was Clive.

"Yeah, I saw it. We look so young."

"That were that goal you scored against Chat'am that won us the game in the last minute, remember?"

"Sure I remember," I lied.

"You got both goals in that game, didn't you?"

"Did I?"

"Yeah, best game you ever played for Sheppey United. There were a Gillingham scout there, right?"

"Maybe, I don't remember. I think they watched me a few times."

"God, what I wouldn't give to 'ave gone to Gillingham like what you did. That would have been a dream come true."

"Gillingham were good to me," I said and suddenly it gave me an idea as to how I might be able to pay off the club's debt to Faversham Town,

45

without having to put my hand in my pocket, which was what I had been intending to do if no better solution presented itself.

As soon as I had managed to get Clive off the phone, I rushed up to my room and made a call to Gillingham Football Club. When I eventually managed to speak to the right person I had to spend the next half an hour begging and pleading for them to give us a friendly game. I played every card I could think of. Hadn't I been a good servant to the Gills? Hadn't they earned a hatful of money when they'd sold me on to QPR? Hadn't I organised and played in a friendly against them when I was at Arsenal? And besides, without clubs like Sheppey United, where was the next Billy Steed going to come from? I was offered the Reserves, but I held out for the First Team and in the end I got what I wanted. We agreed on a date on a Wednesday night and I was left to sort things out with Faversham Town. I made a quick call to Faversham and arranged a meeting with the Chairman for that afternoon. He was understandably delighted at the possibility of being paid the money they were owed.

It was only while I was having lunch alone that I thought about Christine again. It wasn't the first time she had stood me up of course. But I promised myself that it would be the last time. But then, I think I had promised myself that before, hadn't I? I'd been sixteen the last time. It was the end of the season I played for Sheppey United. There were rumours around the club that I was going to be signed by Gillingham, but no one from the Gills had spoken to me yet. I had been riding the crest of a wave really, playing football and seeing Christine and of course trying to fit in a little bit of study as my O Levels approached. At fourteen I had transferred to the Grammar School, the one by the park, and every day when school ended I would run to our bench to meet Christine who had left school at sixteen and was doing a college course which finished at three.

After two years at college, Christine got her first job in a neighbouring town and so I used to have to pass our empty bench on the way home, do my homework in a hurry and then head for the station to meet her when she got back at around five thirty. We would walk back through town, chatting, to her house where her mother would feed us and then we'd go up to her room and listen to music and cuddle on the bed. At the weekends, with my dad out drinking, we'd meet in the park and then go back to my house which we had to ourselves. I'd reluctantly tear myself away from her to go to play football, but when I got home I'd always find her waiting in my room, listening to music or just sleeping. She looked so beautiful sleeping.

It was an idyllic time, one that I naively assumed would last forever. But, of course, nothing lasts forever. I hadn't seen our breakup coming. Not at all. It hit me like a sledgehammer. Maybe Christine had subtly been trying to tell me that it was coming and I hadn't read the signs, or hadn't wanted to. The thing that had haunted me for years was just how long she had kept on seeing me when she was no longer in love with me? I hated myself for not having realised that she was unhappy and for not having helped her to break up with me, but I honestly hadn't seen it coming. It happened on a Saturday morning, the first Saturday that I didn't have to play football after the end of the season. I went to the park to meet her as normal and was surprised to find our bench empty. I just sat down, kind of lost, and waited and waited. Eventually, I realised that she wasn't going to come and I worried that something had happened to her. I set off for her house. I could have gone back to my house and telephoned, but that never occurred to me and instead I walked across town as fast as I could.

When I reached her house, I rang the doorbell and waited nervously for an answer. After an age, she finally opened the door. Her face looked puffy and red, as if she'd been crying.

"What's up?" I asked her.

"Sorry," she began, and she raised her eyes to meet mine. It suddenly dawned on me what she was going to say.

"Christine, no," I begged.

"It's over," she whispered.

"It can't be over," I told her, "I don't want it to be over."

"So sorry," she whispered. And slowly she shut the door and left me in utter disbelief there on the doorstep. I rang the bell again but I knew she wasn't going to answer. After another three rings I finally gave up and slipped away. I was choking back the tears, desperately trying not to lose it there in her street, in her part of town. Head bowed, I stumbled back the way I had come, across the sloping rec and over the waste ground, where the local louts liked to hang out, through the housing estate and finally back to my side of town. Only then did I let my first tears escape, just a few. But it wasn't until I reached the safety of the park and our bench that I really let go. And sitting there on our bench by the Grammar School, head in hands, I cried my heart out. Nothing in life had prepared me for this and I honestly thought I was going to die.

How long I stayed there I don't know. It was definitely more than an hour, probably more than two, maybe even three. Eventually, when the flow of tears began to subside, I became aware that I was soaking wet. At first, I thought I had cried so much that I had somehow drenched myself in tears, but then I realised that it had started to rain heavily. And there I sat, in the rain, in my cleanest T-shirt and only jeans, wretched and unloved, wracking my brain, trying to think of what it was that I had said or done to make Christine no longer love me. We hadn't had an argument or anything, in fact we'd never argued in all the years we'd been together. We'd always wanted the same thing, just to be together. What could I possibly have done? And then the second thought that came into my mind was could there be someone else? Had she got bored with her boyhood sweetheart and decided to finally leave him for someone her own age or maybe older. I thought I could ring her up and ask her, but what if it were true? Did I really want to know? I decided that I didn't, and so, reluctantly, I headed home, a broken-hearted drowned rat.

When I got home I was surprised to find my father there and sober and obviously excited about something. He had been watching Grandstand and sipping at a can of supermarket cola which must have tasted like sewage water to him.

"There you are son, at last. Where you bin all day?"

"Out," I said.

"Well, you're 'ere now. Listen, got a phone call this mornin' from Gilling'am. They wanna take you on for next season. How 'bout that?"

I just looked at him in disbelief. I had been bogged down in the worst day of my life, and now this. At another moment I might have been happy, but it had come at totally the wrong time.

"Christine dumped me," I informed him and I pushed past him and went upstairs to my room and resumed my crying exactly where I had left off in the park, hugging my pillow which of course smelled of her shampoo, wrapped in my duvet which of course felt as soft as her plump breasts.

I didn't go to school on the Monday, instead my dad took me to Gillingham on the train. He chattered incessantly the whole journey about how he had always known that I would be a professional, about how I should learn about football for a couple of years in the youth team and then the reserves and maybe, if I trained hard, I might eventually make the first team. I let it all wash over my head. I wasn't very interested. I didn't want to spend two years in the youth team and then a couple more years in the reserves, what was the point in that? I just wanted to carry on playing for Sheppey United, but more than anything, I wanted to carry on seeing Christine. For me the two went hand in hand.

We were met at the club's offices in Redfern Avenue by the Youth Team Manager who was expecting us, and we were ushered deeper beneath the main stand to an office where, to my father's surprise, the First Team Manager was waiting for us. He shook my father's hand and we sat down in front of his desk. My father was fidgety and nervous but I just couldn't bring myself to care. It was the Youth Team Manager who spoke.

"Well, Mr. Steed, what we 'ave in mind is a two year Youth Contract. Your son will live in the club boarding house in Rainham, attend Rainham Mark Grammar if his O Level grades turn out as predicted and train Tuesday and Thursday Evenings. Matches are Saturday mornings and then 'e's free to go 'ome 'til Sunday night. 'Ow does that sound?"

"Sounds fine," responded my father. "What about wages?"

"I ain't playing in no Youth Team," I said.

"What?" asked the Youth Team Manager.

"What?" echoed my father in utter disbelief.

"I ain't wasting two years playing in no Youth Team."

"You need to learn your trade," said my father, "they'll teach you 'ow to be a good professional." I could see his eyes filled with anger. He was seriously worried that I was going to blow the deal. And yes, I was behaving like an arrogant little shit, and no, I didn't care if I blew the deal. At that moment I hated the whole world and everything in it, and I was ready to go to war with anyone, including my father, no, especially my fucking father.

"It's al'right," my father said addressing the other two men, "he ain't thinking straight."

"Let 'im speak," said the First Team Manager cutting my father off. I raised my head and looked at the man who sat across the big desk from me. He gave me just the hint of a smile.

"I played thirty-eight games this season. Didn't miss one. I scored twenty-one goals from full-back. I can play left or right side, it doesn't bother me. I like playin' for Sheppey United. You want me to leave then you've gotta offer me more than the Youth Team."

"You don't seriously expect to walk straight into the Reserve side at sixteen, do you?" asked the Manager.

"Reserves?" I almost exploded. "I ain't comin' 'ere to play in no Reserves."

"Shut up son, please," begged my father who was watching my professional career float out of the window and away forever.

"So, what do you want?" asked the Manager, no doubt amused by my sheer cheek.

"I'll live in the boarding house. I'll go to Rain'am Mark. I'll do me studies. But, on Wednesday mornings I don't go to school, I train with the First Team. I won't play for no Youth Team on Saturdays or no Reserves on Wednesdays, but I will play for the First Team, if selected." I looked at the Manager and waited for him to throw us out. How many other sixteen year old kids had come into this office and said what I had said? My dad let out a loud sigh. He knew the game was up.

"I admire your spirit son," said the First Team Manager, trying not to laugh, "but you can't seriously expect to get into the First Team at sixteen."

"I'll be seventeen next season, that's old enough. 'Ave you seen me play?" I asked him.

"No, I ain't," he confessed.

"You seen me play?" I asked the Youth Team Manager.

"Yeah, several times."

"Then tell 'im 'ow good I am." I expected the Youth Team Manager to just laugh at me, but he didn't.

"'E's good," he said quietly.

"'Ow good?" asked the First Team Manager.

"Very good. Best sixteen year old I've ever seen in me life. 'E could go all the way."

"Good enough to play in our League Side next season?"

"Yeah, probably, with a bit of work."

"Then why ain't I seen 'im play? Jesus Christ. Okay son, you've got your deal. When do you finish your exams?"

"End of June," said my father.

"Okay, keep yourself fit and you can start pre-season training with the First Team."

"What 'bout wages?" asked my father, and the three of them launched into a discussion about money which held no interest for me whatsoever, and so I switched off and thought about Christine and tried not to burst into tears. They finally agreed on a figure and we waited in reception while a contract was drawn up. I signed about half an hour later. The rest, as they say, is history.

I never saw Christine again, not until the other day in the library. I never got to tell her that I had signed for Gillingham. I never got to tell her that I got ten O Levels. I never got to tell her that I was moving to Rainham. I often thought about calling her and begging her to be just friends, but I knew in my heart that that wasn't going to work. How could I possibly see Christine and not want to kiss her? Anyway, local rumour had it that she had run off with a lorry driver and wasn't even in town anymore. And so I became a footballer.

Bob, the Chairman of Sheppey United, picked me up from my hotel and we drove over to Faversham along the A2. He was very excited at the prospect of the forthcoming friendly against Gillingham and relieved at not having to write out a cheque for five grand to pay off the club's debt before the new season started. I hadn't mentioned to him that I was thinking about paying it off. Faversham Town's ground was next to the A2 in Salters Lane, and it wasn't much changed from how I remembered it. I'd played a friendly there for Sheppey Reserves so that the First Team Manager could see me play for real and convince himself that I really was worth a place in the Southern League side. Clive had played too, and after the match we were told that we were both being promoted to the senior squad. A week later we had sat nervously together on the bench at Sittingbourne's Bull Ground, where Sainsbury's is today, waiting for a taste of First Team action in the last friendly before the start of the league season. I only had to wait twenty minutes as our right back pulled a hamstring and I got my debut. Clive came on in the second half to play right midfield just in front of me and it was the beginning of a fruitful partnership.

The Faversham Chairman was waiting for us in the car park and he unlocked the gates to let us into the ground. We walked around the edge of the pitch to the clubhouse and sat there to talk. Things seemed to be going okay, we agreed on the Wednesday night date for the friendly with Gillingham which we hoped would clear the outstanding debt between our clubs, but then the Chairman of Faversham informed us that we wouldn't be able to play our matches for the coming season at Slaters Lane because they had agreed a deal with someone else. He apologised but said that there had been rumours about Sheppey United being wound up and what with the debt we already had and the near zero attendances of the previous few seasons, he didn't see the sense in us continuing to play there. Especially as we were now a division lower.

We begged and pleaded but to no avail. A deal had already been done with Teynham he said and money had been paid up front, there was no way back. Bob and I left in a state of shock. Sheppey United had been dealt a mortal blow and we both knew it. To all intents and purposes it seemed that our friendly with Gillingham would be my one and only real game as a manager. How were we going to tell the players that we had nowhere to play? The Chairman felt that he had let me down, but I told him not to worry, that I'd think of something, but I wasn't really very optimistic.

Back in my hotel room, I called Clive to tell him the bad news and then I went down to the bar to get shit-faced. It had been a bad day. First Christine had stood me up and now this. It was the kind of day that almost made you want to be back in prison.

In the bar, I was recognised by a group of businessmen who were staying the night at the hotel, and so, fortunately, I didn't have to get drunk alone. They wanted to know about my time at Arsenal and what it was like to play for your country. They took photos with their mobiles with their arms around my shoulders to show their wives that they had met someone famous and then I climbed the stairs to my little attic room and crashed out on the bed fully clothed.

FIVE

I was awoken mid-morning by the annoying ringing of the phone too close to my head to ignore. I felt like shit.

"Yeah?" I asked.

"Hey mate, it's me," said Clive's voice, sounding far too cheerful and far too loud.

"What the fuck d'you want? What time is it?"

"Sounds like you 'ad a heavy night last night," he laughed.

"Don't remember."

"Anyways, get yourself dressed. I've got a solution to our ground problem."

"I am dressed," I said looking down at myself and realising that I still had my clothes on.

"Well, get your arse over 'ere, quick as you can. Call me when you get to Sheerness." I quickly scribbled down his mobile number and told myself for the thousandth time that I ought to get myself a mobile too, everyone had one. It was just that the mobile phone revolution had occurred whilst I was in prison, and to be honest, I felt a bit scared of all this modern stuff, you know, mobile phones and laptops, MP3s and shit.

I showered, shaved and brushed my teeth a couple of times and finally set off for the station. I was getting fed up with taking the train over to the island, but I had never learnt to drive having lived all my adult life in London. I had always moved about by bus or tube in the early days and then by taxi when I became famous and had more money than I knew what to do with. As I walked past St Michael's Church towards the station I thought about all the things I hadn't done in life. I hadn't owned a mobile phone, I hadn't learnt to drive. I hadn't owned my own house and I hadn't got married and had kids. I guess my hangover was making me feel sorry for myself. There were millions of blokes who would give anything to have lived the life I had. Okay, maybe without the seven-year prison stint, and here was I just wanting to be normal, whatever that was.

The little branch line train was waiting, it always was, waiting for the fast train to London to arrive and then for the fast train going the other way, to the coast. Then it would wait on still, for the slow trains, one going in each direction, and only then would it finally be allowed to leave.

I rang Clive from the phone box outside Sheerness station and ten minutes later he arrived to pick me up in a brand spanking new minibus. He pulled up at the front of the station and jumped out.

"'Ave you seen it?" he asked, pointing at the side of the minibus. "Picked it up yesterday."

The minibus had Clive's Coaches, proud sponsors of Sheppey United FC painted in bright red along the side.

"You're gonna look pretty stupid drivin' 'round in that when Sheppey United don't exist no more," I told him.

"I ain't gonna let that 'appen mate. 'Ere, there's someone I want ya to meet," and he pointed to the inside of his bus. I climbed into the minibus and saw Clive Junior sitting there with another lad who I had never seen before. He was remarkably tall and thin, taller and thinner even than Charlie Chalk.

"Billy Steed, meet our new goalie, Barry Branch," said Clive sounding very pleased with himself. I reached across to shake the hand of our newest recruit. It was a big hand too, this kid looked like a goalie.

"Al'right mate," I said and it was a big relief to finally have a keeper.

"'E played with me at Sittin'bourne last year," Clive Junior told me.

"Didn't play that much," Barry told me.

"'E were kinda reserve keeper," said Clive helpfully. So, there it was, we had just got ourselves Sittingbourne Reserve's reserve keeper. I almost had to laugh. When I had been a kid, Sheppey had been leagues above Sittingbourne, and now we were grateful for having their second string rejects to be in our first team.

"Don't worry," I told him, "you'll get plenty of action with us."

"Good," he said, "that's why I'm 'ere."

I sat down in the front seat and Clive started the engine. I didn't bother to ask where we were going, he wouldn't have told me anyway. I guessed I'd find out soon enough. To my surprise, we started heading away from Sheerness. I found myself wondering if Clive had done a deal with some farmer out in the sticks to let us play in his sheep field or something. I was relieved when we reached Half Way and turned onto the gravel track that led to the Stevedore's Sports Ground. I had been there years before to see my dad play cricket, and when we neared the gate to the pitch we saw that it was still set up for cricket, the square roped off in the middle of the field. Clive parked the minibus and we got out to wait for whoever it was that we had come to meet. A familiar silver BMW arrived and drew up next to the minibus.

Ten minutes later, the groundsman turned up with a smartly-dressed middle-aged man who introduced himself as the President of the Stevedore's Club. We went into the ground for a tour of the facilities. I don't think the president realised just how desperate we were for somewhere to play, or maybe he was just very proud of his club and wanted to show it off. There was a small clubhouse like a nissen hut which had a bar and entertainment area with a small stage, and then close by were the changing rooms. It was a thousand times better than the sheep field I had been imagining.

The groundsman explained that there was no seating area for fans, but that in the league we were going to be in that wasn't expected. In fact, fans weren't expected. As long as one side of the pitch was roped off, just in case anyone did turn up to watch that was all that was required. They even had portable managers/substitutes dugouts which were stored away but would be brought out in time for the start of the season.

"'Ow much we gonna be charged?" asked Bob.

"We don't 'ave to pay a thing," put in Clive. "It's all sorted out." Of course Clive had his business nearby and knew everyone in Half Way.

"We put one of our members on the gate and charge a small entry fee to those who come to watch," said the Stevedore's President. "And, we open the clubhouse during and after games for refreshments."

"Really?" questioned Bob.

"Yeah, we think there's gonna be a lot of interest in Sheppey United this year with Billy Steed as Manager. Besides, I was a fan back in the eighties and I'd like to see the club back playing on the Island. I think everyone would."

"Great," I said before anyone could change their minds. We all shook hands.

"D'you think we could arrange a friendly match with our team?" asked the President.

"Sure," I agreed, "no problem. Let us know when the pitch is ready and we'll hype it up as the long-awaited return of Sheppey United to the Island."

So now we had four pre-season games to look forward to. Four matches to get our team into shape, two games in the prison, the match against Stevedore Sports and of course the big one against Gillingham. It certainly felt like Sheppey United had been given a new lease of life. The sense of relief was enormous.

I was finally getting my life into some sort of routine and routines were good, I'd learnt that in prison. Every morning I would go for a jog as far as the park, do a couple of slow laps just in case Christine showed up, although of course I knew she wouldn't, and then jog back to the hotel for breakfast. After breakfast, I would head into town, sometimes to the library to change books in the hope of seeing Christine again, but she was never there, sometimes to a little café in the Forum from where I could watch the shoppers hurrying past. Didn't Christine ever go shopping?

I would normally have lunch at the Red Lion, just a sandwich and a pint whilst reading the newspaper, and then I would return to the hotel for a sleep. In the afternoon, when I woke up, I would stay in bed reading or watching documentaries for a couple of hours until it was time to go down for dinner. After dinner, I would spend the rest of the evening in the bar, getting drunk in the company of the hotel's transient guests who were mostly surprised and delighted to find an ex-England captain there to talk to.

I know you're thinking that it doesn't sound like much of a life, but when you've been in prison for seven years anything is an improvement. The highlights were Tuesday and Thursday evenings when I got the train over to the island to work with my team at the prison. Things were going okay. The squad was getting on well enough and our passing and control were starting to improve. And we had a keeper. Okay so they'd nicknamed him Marge because everything he had tried to catch in his first session had slipped out, but I had put that down to nerves, and within a couple of weeks he appeared a lot more confident and was coming for crosses and catching them, well, most of the time. I had

Clive working with him a lot. A good team needs a good goalkeeper, since confidence begins at the back and spreads forward. Whilst Clive was busy with Barry Branch, I worked on the other sections of our team. I had Clive Junior earmarked to be captain and to play as the sweeper in our back three. He seemed to like this idea and listened intently to any advice I gave him, after all, when I had belatedly grown to over six foot Arsenal had changed me from a full back to a sweeper, where my pace surprised many a forward bearing down on goal.

I had long ago decided that Ginger would be our holding defensive midfielder. He might look like his legs could break at any moment, but he was strong and determined in a tackle like you wouldn't believe. The only thing I was worried about was whether or not he had the discipline for the role. It was a position that would go largely unnoticed, and I knew that Ginger liked to be the centre of attention. Still, I was working on him. I put in as much time as I could with our two strikers as well. Goals are of course the be all and end all of football. Our two forwards were Chalk and Cheese, yes that was what they were called, although neither name was for real. Charlie Chalk was everyone else's hero, slightly older than the others, doing time already and of course our self-styled star striker. And then there was Andy Cheese, or Cheesy as everyone called him. He was Ginger's best mate, partner in crime and probable future cell-sharer and hadn't played the previous season because he had been in Borstal. He was fairly short, but quick, the perfect foil to lanky Charlie Chalk. We did plenty of shooting practice. I taught Charlie to play with his back to goal and then to turn and shoot, whilst I made Andy always hang on the shoulder of the last defender and trust his pace to get him half a yard which was all he needed to be able to get a shot away. I taught them to shoot hard and low, across the keeper, and I taught them always to follow up each other's shots in case of spills.

When our new kit arrived, I got the sports reporter from the Gazette to meet us at the Stevedore's Ground and we officially announced that this was to be the new home of Sheppey United. The lads finally looked like footballers in their new gear although Charlie Chalk wasn't allowed out for the photo. As soon as the picture was taken, Clive collected the new kit from everyone and carefully counted it back into the bag where it would remain until our first game against the prison guards. Clive and I had decided to give the two games in the prison no publicity at all. Both would be played behind closed doors and would give us the chance to try out our new formation in peace.

The game against the guards took place on a sweltering evening in early August, and although we looked the part in our brand new kit, things didn't go well at all. Charlie Chalk was too pumped up, and I pulled him off after twenty minutes at the referee's insistence. Charlie called me every name he could think of and swore never to play for us again, got changed and disappeared back to his cellblock before it was even half time. The guards had a regular team in the Island Sunday League, so it wasn't as if they had just got together for a one time kick about, even so, I would have hoped that my lads would have given them a good game, but it wasn't to be. We lost 3-0 and our discipline was nowhere to be seen. Our keeper had a nightmare and dropped every cross that came into our box. Ginger Snap went AWOL from the heart of our midfield and left our three-man defence cruelly exposed. The score line could have been a lot more had it not been for some lone heroics from Clive Junior and the fact that the opposition squandered a hatful of chances.

After the game, I returned to the dressing room to find a full-scale argument raging back and forth about who was to blame for our poor performance, but when they saw me come in things soon went quiet. I guess they expected me to start raving at them, to yell and swear and call them all useless, but that wasn't my style. I stood in the middle of the changing room and looked around at my team who sat on the benches, heads bowed, waiting for a tirade.

"Well lads, we've still got a long way to go 'aven't we?" I said quietly.

"Can say that again," said Clive.

"Right, get changed and let's get out of 'ere. There's no point in dwelling on that performance, we'll just forget 'bout it and move on," and I left the changing room. As soon as I was out of the door, I heard the arguments start up again. Clive joined me when he had finished collecting up the kit. Bob, the Chairman, walked over to us having been involved in a conversation with the Prison Governor.

"So, what went wrong?" he asked me.

"Everythin'," I told him honestly enough.

I had two days to ponder our defeat as we were due back at Eastchurch to play the prisoners on the Thursday evening. I must be honest and say that the thought of quitting crossed my mind on several occasions. I spoke to Clive on the phone for over an hour on the Wednesday morning and as we tossed excuses and solutions to and fro so I decided to carry on. This was all new to me. I'd had a spectacular career. I'd won three league titles with Arsenal and played nearly fifty games for my country, over half of them as captain, but I had never been involved with a team of no-hopers before.

At some point during a long and restless night on the Wednesday, somewhere between being awake and being in a nightmare, it occurred to me that my players just didn't expect to win. They had gone the whole of the previous season without tasting victory and they had forgotten how to win. Winning was a habit that you got into. Winning equals confidence. Confidence equals playing better and playing better equals winning. The perfect circle. I had to get these boys a victory from somewhere, I had to somehow make them feel good about themselves. It wasn't going to be easy. I realised that I hadn't known failure in my professional life and that I wasn't equipped to deal with it. My brilliant career had been cut short at its brilliant peek. I had never known what it was like to feel my talent slowly draining away. I had never been dropped from the team to sit and stew on the bench to eventually be free-transferred out. I hadn't gone down the leagues desperate to get a game for anyone who would have me, prison had saved me from all of that. Prison had saved me from the heartache of having to say "that's it, I'm no longer good enough, it's time to call it a day." Maybe prison had robbed me of coming to terms with being ordinary.

SIX

Thursday afternoon, batteries recharged, I got the train over to the island once again. The big question going round and round in my mind was whether or not Charlie Chalk would play. It was the first big test of my man-management skills and I knew that the rest of the squad would want to see how I handled their hero. I hoped that he would just come up to me, apologise, and we could get on with things without a big fuss, but Charlie somehow didn't seem the apologetic type. I didn't really want a stand up dressing room row with him in front of everyone else. That way, if he stormed out, he might take half of the rest with him. I hadn't thought that being a football manager was going to be easy, but we'd only had one kick about match and already we were facing a crisis.

The players arrived in dribs and drabs and the minibus started to fill up. Everyone said "Al'right Boss" to me, but there was an air of unease as we set off for Eastchurch. The players got changed and went out to warm up with Clive, and I sat alone in the changing room, waiting for inspiration to strike for my team talk and hoping that Charlie Chalk might come in. Charlie didn't show. Clive brought the others back in.

"Charlie's playin' for them Boss," Ginger informed me.

"It's true mate," said Clive.

"No big deal," I decided, "we'll just 'ave to do without 'im."

"Want me to play up front Boss?" offered Ginger.

"No. You've gotta prove to me this evenin' that you're disciplined enough to play a holding midfield role, otherwise you won't be starting against Gilling'am." I expected him to argue, but he didn't. I put one of our more attacking midfielders up front and one of the subs from the previous game took his place in the middle of the park.

"Okay, the last match was just a try to get used to the formation and have a laugh game, as from today we start to take things more seriously. And that starts with you Ginger. First time you go wandering up front I'll pull you off, you're only job is to protect our defence. I want everyone to work their socks off out there. This is Sheppey United, wear your shirt with pride. Don't let the team down by being the one who doesn't give 110% out there."

I hadn't mentioned the word "win" but it was what I hoped I had inferred. I let them leave the changing room to face the hostile atmosphere of a game against prisoners inside their own prison. I knew the inmates had a team in the local league just as the guards did, but they were a division lower and should therefore be an easier task for us. Having said that, they now had our star striker playing up front for them.

The game was a rough and tumble affair, not pretty to watch at all, but at least my players matched the opposition for effort. The referee, one of the prison guards, was tough on everything and thus avoided a blood bath, although he gave the prisoners a couple of soft penalties late on, both of which Charlie Chalk converted. And so we lost our final game in the prison 2-0, but at least we had competed this time and our discipline had greatly improved.

I congratulated the lads on a much better performance and went outside to wait for them. Charlie Chalk was there, obviously having decided it was time to talk.

"Al'right Boss," he said quietly.

"Al'right mate, nice couple of penalties."

"Thanks. I did what you taught me the other week," he said modestly. It was true, I'd had a go at penalty taking with him and Cheesy at one of our recent sessions, you know, about making your mind up and not changing it. Easy to say but not so easy to do under pressure.

"So?" I asked.

"So, I'd like to play for you again."

"Okay mate," I told him. I could have demanded an apology in front of the whole team. I could have told him to fuck off that we didn't need him. Instead, I just stuck out a hand for him to shake. He shook it gratefully and then disappeared back towards his cellblock and I waited for Clive to tell him the good news. I had a lot of work to do with Charlie Chalk, but if handled correctly he could definitely be an asset to our squad.

In the week leading up to the game with Gillingham, I went into publicity overdrive. I knew at first hand the power of the press and I was determined, on this occasion, to use it to my club's advantage.

Gillingham had promised to at least start some of their younger first team players and we billed the game accordingly.

I had persuaded Bob, the Chairman, that the way to drum up support was for me to go around the local schools and to give out free tickets to the kids provided they entered the ground with a paying adult. We talked with Faversham and arranged for drinks and pies and hotdogs and stuff, which I knew would make us more money than entry fees. The club bar would stay open after the match too, and that would certainly increase the profits.

I rang round the local schools from Teynham, Sittingbourne, Faversham and Rainham, and most agreed to allow me to go to talk to their pupils. It was only a little twenty minute talk with ten minutes or so for questions at the end, which meant I could get through three or four schools a day in the same town. I started in Rainham at my old school where I was of course a legend, despite everything that had happened. My talk was about working hard at what you wanted to do, about achieving your goals through dedication and never accepting failure. I filled it in with a few anecdotes about the different clubs I had played for and of course a few England stories. I told them what it was like to win three league titles, and what it felt like to wear the three lions in a World Cup Finals – I'd played in two. I didn't tell them the real story of my career. I didn't say that if I hadn't been born with an exceptional natural talent that I would never have made it. I didn't tell them that I had always hated training and did my best to avoid it. And of course I didn't tell them about the loneliness and the endless hotel rooms or about the gambling and alcohol or about how I got stripped of the England captaincy in disgrace and did seven years in prison. At the end of the talk, I handed the Head of PE a bag full of free match tickets and a signed poster and then moved onto the next school.

In Sittingbourne, I started with the boy's grammar school, the one next to the park, the one I had been to for three years from fourteen to sixteen years old. I'd given away a last minute penalty that had lost us the game in the Under 14 Kent Cup Final which we'd played at Priestfield Stadium the home of Gillingham, and I'd always felt guilty about that. Almost as guilty as I felt about missing that penalty that got England eliminated from my last World Cup. Everyone remembers that.

It was in the afternoon, at a junior school on the other side of town, when after my talk, slightly reduced for younger audiences who didn't really know who I was, a small boy came up to me.

"You're the bloke from the library, ain't ya?" said the boy. I looked at him and although I didn't recognise him I guessed that he must be Christine's son.

"Yeah. And Christine's your mum, right?"

"Yeah. My granddad said it's true, you used to be captain of Arsenal. 'E said you used to be friends with my mum."

"I am friends with your mum," I told him.

"So, you wanna come round for tea? I've got a goal in my garden. We can play football with my granddad."

"I'd like that," I said.

"Come along Billy," called out a young blonde teacher who assumed that the boy was annoying me and that I had somewhere more important to be.

"Your name's Billy?" I asked the boy when I realised that she wasn't talking to me.

"Yeah, we've got the same name," he told me.

"Wow, that's a coincidence."

The teacher walked over to us.

"Sorry Mr. Steed," she said.

"It's okay, I know the boy's mother," I told her.

"Oh, okay then." And she left us alone.

"So, are you gonna come watch my team play against Gilling'am?" I asked him.

"I'd like to," he said.

"Tell your dad to take you," I told him.

"I ain't got a dad," he replied.

"Your granddad than?"

"'E's not well at the moment."

"Well, your mum."

"She don't like football."

"True. Okay you can come with me, 'ow does that sound?"

"Great," agreed the boy, his eyes wide with excitement.

"Well, I'll need to talk to your mum, but if she says it's okay then we'll pick you up in the team bus. You can sit in the dugout with me. Al'right?"

"Brilliant."

"Do you know your mum's phone number?" I asked him.

"Sure," he said, and I wrote it down on the back of the piece of paper I had with my speech notes on.

"I'll call 'er and ask if it's okay for you to come." I gave the boy a signed poster of me in my England shirt. I liked the idea of Christine seeing it every time she went into her son's bedroom. Of course it was me from ten years before, a bit thinner, a bit more hair, no grey at the temples. Me in my prime. Captain of my country. Three lions on my heart and the world at my feet. I could have signed for Barcelona or Milan and maybe I should have. My decision to stay at Arsenal just led to a whole heap of trouble.

After the talk at the last school of the day, I walked back through town and passing a phone shop I finally decided to buy my first mobile. Welcome to the twenty-first century Billy Steed, at last. The girl in the shop tried to impress me with words like roaming, GPS, Bluetooth, megapixels and a lot of other complicated crap, but when she realised that I was having a hard time following her, she showed me a very basic 'open and it's on' model.

"'Ave you got it in red?" I asked.

"Only black," she replied no doubt impressed by my in depth technical knowledge of colours. And so I had a mobile phone, a black one. I topped up twenty quid as the girl in the shop suggested, and then I hurried to my hotel room to read the instructions so that I could ring Christine. Only an hour later and I was ready to make my first call. I nervously punched in the number and pressed the green telephone icon button to ring the call. I had to remember to press the red telephone button when I finished the call. It started to ring. I held my breath. Christine answered.

"Hey Christine, it's Billy," I shouted.

"Hi Billy. You don't 'ave to shout."

"Sorry," I said, "first mobile phone experience."

"Listen, 'bout the other day, I'm really sorry. My dad's been ill and I couldn't face goin' out. I should've called the 'otel."

"It's okay. Sorry 'bout your dad."

"'E seems to be a bit better now."

"That's good."

"I didn't tell you, but I moved back in with my parents a few months ago. I lost my job and, well, y'know."

"I know. Things'll get better."

"You reckon?" she laughed.

"Oh yeah, trust me," I said.

"So, you wanted to take my son to a football match."

"'E told ya?"

"'E's talked 'bout nothing else since I picked 'im up from school."

"So, what d'you say?"

"Ain't he gonna be a bit of a burden?"

"Nah, don't worry. I'll 'ave to get everyone to watch their language, that's all."

"If it ain't no bother. You remember the house, don't you?"

"Of course I do. We'll pick 'im up at seven."

"Fine. I'll tell 'im." There was a pause as if the conversation was over.

"You didn't tell me you called your son Billy," I blurted out before she said goodbye.

"'Is father left me when I was pregnant. 'E always 'ated it that I was Billy Steed's Ex. So I named his son after you. That really pissed 'im off. Anyways, Billy ain't your real name, you don't own it."

"Course not. They called me Billy at Sheppey after my dad."

"I 'eard when your dad died."

"'E just never got over my mum leavin' im."

"Did you ever 'ear from 'er?"

"Never. Maybe she's dead too. Anyway, let's not talk about that."

We said goodbye and said we'd see each other at her parents' house on Wednesday before the game when I picked up her son. I remembered to press the red button to end the call, and my first mobile phone experience was over. I breathed a sigh of relief that I hadn't said anything too stupid and went down to dinner.

On the Wednesday evening, Clive picked me up in the minibus from outside the hotel and we drove across town to get Christine's son. The lads in the bus chattered excitedly about their match with Gillingham, but I was only excited about seeing Christine. We stopped outside the house in a little side street off the Canterbury Road, and I saw the boy and his granddad waiting for us in the porch. The same porch were I'd kissed Christine goodbye so many times before I went home of a night. The house was unchanged. Christine appeared at the door and waved. I got out of the minibus and went to shake hands with her dad.

"Looking well," I told him, although he looked like death.

"Thanks. Look at you after all these years. I used to watch you on the tele playing for Ars'nal and for England of course. I could 'ardly believe it was you."

"It was me al'right," I told him. "Well, we'd better get going."

"Come in for a beer after if y'like," he offered.

"I dunno," I said and I looked at Christine for guidance. She gave me a quick smile and so I agreed to stop when we brought the boy back. I led Little Billy to the minibus and got him settled in a seat and he waved goodbye to his mother and grandfather as we pulled away.

When we got to the ground, the lads got changed and went out to warm up. I produced a brand new small-sized white football from my kit bag and handed it to the boy.

"It's for you," I told him, "let's go see 'ow good you are."

I took him out onto the pitch and we kicked the ball back and forth between us for a bit. The ground was starting to fill up and it looked like my publicity drive was going to pay off. You could smell the hotdogs and hamburgers and hear the excited chatter of schoolboy voices. It was the kind of evening I would have liked to have attended with my father, but when I was a child the only spare cash my dad had was invested in the local brewery. He worked on and off at the pie factory. Sometimes he reached supervisor before being sacked for turning up drunk, but they always took him back after a couple of months when he was desperate enough to go and beg. He was always happy to start again at the bottom of the ladder. He once switched to the paper mill, and doubled his salary and convinced himself that things were finally going to get better, but he never adapted to the shift pattern. Having to work at weekends was killing him and three months later he was back making pies. I lived on pies when I was a kid, our freezer was always full of them. They had no labels or anything, you just took pot luck, put one in the oven for twenty minutes, and then when you cut into it you discovered if it was steak and kidney, chicken and mushroom or, god forbid, vegetable, yuck! When I left home and had to fend for myself I still lived on pies from the local chippie, but I padded out my diet with the odd portion of chips, I could afford it. Pies were the reason Christine used to invite me to her house to eat so much, maybe she didn't care for them quite like I did, or maybe she thought I needed some sort of variety in my diet. Her mum always complained how skinny I was and seemed to make it her personal mission to fatten me up. She didn't succeed. I'm just one of those people who can eat what they like and never get fat, lucky I guess, I personally put it down to my childhood pie diet. Maybe you should try it?

Little groups of boys began to come onto the pitch and cluster around the better-known Gillingham players to get their autographs. Then, one of them recognised me from a talk I had done at his school and a group formed around me as well. I called Clive over to look after Little Billy for a bit and busied myself signing autographs.

When the match got underway, I took the boy to the dugout with me and we sat and watched my team being toyed with. Gillingham were deliberately kind to us, just moving the ball about as if they were on the training ground. Every now and then with a blinding change of pace one of them would race away from our defence and slot the ball past our helpless keeper, almost at regular intervals. The crowd cheered everything they did. By half time they had scored five.

For the second half, the Gills withdrew their first team players and the match wasn't quite as one-sided as before. Even so, with a couple of minutes remaining they were 8-0 ahead. It was then that Cheesy finally managed to get in our first shot on goal. The keeper saved it but then spilled it right at the feet of Charlie Chalk who bundled it over the line for the biggest cheer of the night. Little Billy sitting beside me cheered and cheered and I was afraid he would lose his voice.

The game ended and we went to the bar for a quick drink before heading home. I realised that none of my team had made a move to get served and it occurred to me that they didn't have the money to buy themselves a drink, so I went to the bar and bought them all a pint or a coke or whatever they wanted. Little Billy sipped an orange juice and munched his way through a packet of cheese and onion crisps. He'd had a burger just after half time, so it wasn't as if I would be taking him home hungry or anything.

When we were finished in the bar we set off back along the A2 and Clive dropped me outside Christine's house.

"See you on Saturday," I said to Clive as I carried the boy off the bus in my arms since he had fallen fast asleep during the short journey. Christine had been waiting for our return, and opened the front door for me. She led me up the stairs to Billy's room and I placed him gently on his bed beneath the poster I had given him and prized his new football from his arms and put it down on the floor. Christine tugged off his trainers and left him in his tracksuit, pulling the covers over him.

"'E behave himself?" she whispered.

"'E was good as gold," I told her.

"My dad went to bed, 'e was too tired. 'E said to say sorry. But mum's downstairs, she'd like to see ya."

"That'd be nice."

We went downstairs together and into the kitchen. When she heard us Christine's mum came through from the living room.

"Oh my god!" she exclaimed, "look at you!" and she hugged me to her like I was some returned prodigal son.

"Nice to see you," I said when she finally released me.

"You look so different, so tall, so strong."

"I was only a boy when you knew me."

And so we sat and talked, Christine brought me a beer. And, for me at least, it was as if twenty years had never passed and here we were again on a typical night after tea, sitting around the dining room table, talking. After a while, Christine's mum excused herself and left us alone. Christine brought me another beer and sipped at a glass of water, and so suddenly we were alone together for the first time for so long, and I'd imagined this for seven endless years in prison every night, and never dared to dream that it might one day happen. There was a silence. I guess neither of us knew where to start. Eventually, I asked her about the other three children who I hadn't met yet and she talked a bit about having three teenage girls in the house. I couldn't begin to imagine what the queue for the bathroom was like in the mornings. She talked quietly for a while and I was happy just to listen to her voice, her actual words were unimportant. How many nights had I dreamt of hearing that voice again?

When she ran out of things to tell me about her children she asked me what plans I had for the future. I just laughed.

"I don't make plans. I'm just happy to be out of prison. Every day's like a holiday."

"You can't live in a 'otel for the rest of your life," she said.

"Can't I?"

"No, it must be costin' a fortune."

"I've got money."

"You won't 'ave for long if you keep livin' in a 'otel."

"It's only the Coniston. It ain't the Ritz or nothing."

"Still must be costin' you a packet, unless the club pays."

"What? Sheppey United? You're joking. They don't even pay me a wage."

"You mean you're working for nothin'?"

"Yeah, the club's bankrupt. We played that game tonight to try and pay off some debts. There's no money for wages. The players don't get match expenses. Clive provides the transport and he bought the kit too. I bought some footballs and the Chairman has promised to pay our league and registration fees for a year. We're going to play at the Stevedore's ground at Half Way for free and we train at Eastchurch prison, again for free."

"You're crazy. 'Ow can you work for nothin'?"

"'Cause no one else would 'ave me Christine," I told her hoping that I didn't sound too pathetic.

"You was England captain."

"I was disgraced remember. I got sentenced to ten years in prison. I was lucky an' I got out early, but it don't mean I've bin forgiven."

"But you were innocent John." She whispered and she gently took my hand. It was the first time anyone had called me by my real name for as long as I could remember, and it was the first time she had held my hand for twenty years, and for a moment I thought I was going to cry.

"What makes you think I was innocent?" I asked her, a lump in my throat that felt like a tennis ball.

"I know you," she said. And of course she did. She knew me better than I knew myself. At first in prison, I had clung to my innocence and a firm belief that justice would be done and that I would be released, but as the days became months and the appeals floundered, so I lost faith in the system, and maybe even I began to doubt my own innocence. After the first year, I just accepted the situation, once I realised that by the time I got out I was going to be too old to ever play top level football again it just didn't seem to matter anymore whether I was innocent or guilty. I did my time. I kept myself reasonably fit and I studied hard for my coaching badges which I took as soon as I was released.

She was still holding my hand. It felt good.

"Better go," I told her, although I could have stayed that way all night.

"Want me to give you a lift back to the 'otel?" she offered.

"It's al'right, I like to walk."

"It's a long way."

"I've got things to think about. The walk will do me good."

"If you're sure." She showed me to the door.

"It was nice talking," I told her.

"Yeah. Just like old times. Thanks for taking Billy to the game."

"My pleasure."

"I'll call you for that coffee."

"It's al'right, you don't 'ave to say things you don't mean."

"No, I mean it. I'd like to talk again."

"Well, you've got my number."

"I'll call you."

"Sure."

"I will John." I looked into her eyes and I saw that she was serious. I wanted to ask her why she had dumped me all those years ago, but more than that I wanted to kiss her. We were on her doorstep. We'd always kissed goodbye on that doorstep. I remember when we were kids as we kissed goodbye she would sometimes whisper in my ear that she wasn't wearing a bra and I would put my cold hands up her jumper and hold her warm breasts as we kissed. This time I tore myself away and half way down the road I turned and waved, she waved back.

The night wasn't cold, just a bit autumnal as befitted the last week in August, but it was perfect for walking. I headed for the main A2 and the long way back to the hotel. It was after midnight and there was no one around.

Somewhere along the High Street I saw the brightly-lit window of an estate agents and I stopped to look at what was for sale. And there was my old house in the window, unloved and unwanted. I guess I knew how it felt.

SEVEN

Saturday 2nd September was our last friendly before the start of the league season. Our last chance to come to terms with my formation before things became important. We were playing the Stevedore's Club at what was now our shared ground and a small crowd had turned up in response to an article in the local paper about the long-awaited return of Sheppey United to the Island. I hoped that the following Saturday might bring a few more fans for our first home league match.

We didn't have Charlie Chalk since he wasn't allowed out for such a minor game, but we started brightly enough and raced into a two-nil lead by half time. I was pleased by the way things were going and knew how much a victory would mean to my team, but in the second half, for no apparent reason, the players seemed to doubt themselves and our opponents came back to draw two all, still, it was better than another defeat. I felt reasonably happy that with the extra fire-power of Charlie Chalk up front we would be more of a force to be reckoned with in the coming weeks.

We trained at the prison on the Tuesday and Thursday evenings of the following week as usual. The squad seemed in good spirits and there was a pleasing togetherness about the whole thing. We played two-touch five-a-side for a lot of the time, and I realised just how well we were keeping the ball compared to what we had been like when I had first taken over. I was beginning to feel quietly confident about things, but that illusive first win was still playing on my mind. The sooner that came the better.

I dedicated the last few days before the big opening day of the season to going around the Island schools to drum up support, just as I had done on the mainland before the Gillingham game. It had worked once, so hopefully it would work again, although the allure of Betteshanger Welfare wasn't quite in the same bracket as that of the Gills.

Bob, the Chairman, picked me up from the station before the match. Charlie Chalk was already on board, snoozing like a baby in the back. That was one thing you learnt to do in prison, sleep. It was a great way to escape and it helped pass the time. I didn't disturb him by saying hello, I just got into the front and we headed for Half Way.

"So Billy, this is the big one," said the Chairman.

"The first big one," I told him.

When we arrived at the ground we found Clive already there waiting for us. I could tell he was nervous as he sprang out of his new minibus and bounded across the car park towards us.

"Hi mate," he said, "this is the big one."

"Relax Clive, it's just another game of football. The start of a long season."

"Ain't you nervous?" he wanted to know.

"Nah, course not," I lied. "I played in the Nou Camp with 130,000 fans booing my every touch because I'd turned down a move to Barcelona the previous summer, now that can make you nervous."

He nodded as if he knew what I meant and took a deep breath.

"Go to the changing room and 'ang the kit up," I told him, I knew he needed something to do. I left the others and walked out across the pitch. The ground was hard and the sun was shining in a clear blue sky, it was going to be a tough game. I'd have to get Clive filling up water bottles when I got to the changing rooms.

The reporter from the local paper appeared and walked across to me. We shook hands.

"First game of the season. Fink you can start wiv a win mate?"

"That's what we're 'ere to do," I told him.

"Only the champions get promoted. That what you're aiming for?"

"Absolutely." I excused myself and headed back across the pitch. I glanced nervously towards the car park to see if I could spot our players' cars, wondering if they had been able to make the two minute journey out from Sheerness. It was then that I noticed a little boy waving at me. It was Christine's son and he was busily tugging at his grandfather's hand, hauling the old man towards the gate where someone from the Stevedore's Club was taking entry money and handing out printed team sheets. I hurried over. A little way off I saw Christine locking her car.

"Hi there," I called out as I got closer.

"I brought me football," shouted Little Billy holding it up for me to see, "we gonna have a kick about?"

"Course we are," I told him.

"Hi," said Christine as she reached us. "'E's talked of nothin' but football since you took 'im to that match, so my dad decided we should bring 'im over today."

"That's great," I said. I dipped into my pocket and handed the man on the gate a few quid to cover their entry fee and walked with them across to the roped-off area for spectators. I took Billy's hand and led him out onto the pitch and we kicked about a bit. A screech of brakes from the car park and the sound of crunching gravel told me that Ginger and his mates had finally arrived. I left the boy with his mother and grandfather and headed off to the changing rooms. It was time to start work in earnest.

The small crowd got behind our team and urged us forward and the players responded accordingly. We took a deserved lead after half an hour when Ginger slotted a nice pass through to Cheesy and he rounded the keeper with nonchalant ease. In the second half we kept pressing forward looking for more goals, but the Betteshanger defence held out well. With twenty minutes left the opposition decided to ruin the party and scored a breakaway goal that they didn't really deserve. And so the match looked as if it was heading for a draw, until the last minute when the linesman missed a blatant offside and Betteshanger grabbed an unlikely winner. At the final whistle I saw some of my players heading for the referee to protest about the late goal and I ran over and shepherded them off the pitch. Harassing match officials was not part of my philosophy.

In the changing room, the lads showered and changed and moaned about their bad luck. I let them get on with things until they were all ready to leave and then I sat them down on the benches.

"I'm glad that you're all pissed off," I told them. "You should be."

"Yeah, we was robbed," said Ginger.

"No, you should be pissed off with yourselves for letting a last minute goal affect the result. If we had taken just a few of our chances then this game would have been out of sight by half time. We could have scored six or seven. That way we wouldn't have cared about a last minute goal. That's the lesson I want you to learn from today, when you're on top of a team you 'ave to turn your domination into goals."

"We'll win the next one," said Clive Junior and there was a chorus of agreement.

"Good," I concluded, "I'll see you all Tuesday for training." And I went to leave.

"Boss, hey, don't we get a pint today?" asked Ginger.

"No, you can think of a drink after the game as your win bonus. No win. No bonus. Try 'arder next time."

Outside, I looked to see if Christine might be waiting for me. Her car was still there, so I headed for the clubhouse and found her seated at a table with her father and son. I asked what I could get them to drink and headed for the bar. As I got back to their table with a tray of drinks, I saw my team making their way back to their cars. I felt a twinge of guilt about not buying them a drink, but if the promise of an after-match beer would inspire them in future games then I had to use it. Yes, they'd been unlucky, but no we didn't have any points yet.

The Chairman came over after a while and asked if I needed a lift back to the station as he was going to take Charlie Chalk back to the prison.

"Come wiv us," offered Christine, and so I stayed. I knew Bob was disappointed with the result, but he hadn't said anything. He had hoped that I could perform miracles with his little team, but now he would have to face the fact that I was just human after all. I personally tried to look on the bright side, I still had another twenty-three goes at winning a league game.

Christine drove us back to Sittingbourne, it was her dad's car but he didn't feel strong enough to drive yet. Standing to watch the match had left him understandably shattered. We parked outside the house and Little Billy and his grandfather disappeared inside.

"Shall I take you back?" offered Christine.

"What about if we get somethin' to eat?" I suggested.

"Okay, where?"

"I saw a Mexican the other night, where Hulbards used to be. 'Ow 'bout that?"

"Sounds good, I'll just let mum know." She got out of the car and I followed her.

"Wait in the car if you want," said Christine.

"No, besides, let's walk into town."

"Okay sure."

When Christine finally re-emerged from the house, I saw that she had changed clothes and done her makeup, but to me she always looked beautiful, whatever. We set off walking slowly into town along the busy A2 and she slipped her arm into mine. It felt natural enough, like we were once again two dizzy teenagers out on a date. We didn't say much, neither of us was a big talker.

After I walked Christine home at the end of the night, and resisted the temptation to kiss her on her doorstep, I stopped once more at the brightly-lit window of the estate agents that had my house in the window. The thought of buying it had been nagging away at my brain since I'd first seen the For Sale sign in the front garden and I knew I wasn't going to be able to resist much longer. I wanted to give the house to Christine so that she could live in it with her children, but I knew she would never accept it. Besides, she was out of work and wouldn't be able to pay the bills and was never going to let me pay them for her. Still, I could buy the house for myself and then try to work out a way of getting Christine to live there. Perhaps, when she found a job, she might take it in exchange for a minimal rent. Me personally, I liked living in hotels, or at least it was all I knew.

The next morning I found myself entering the estate agents. The man there sitting at his computer saw me, did a double take, and suddenly bounded to his feet as if he had received an electric shock.

"My god! It's Billy Steed. Al'right?" he half shouted so that his secretary knew the importance of who had just casually happened in off the street. When he reached me, he pumped my hand enthusiastically.

"Al'right," I said.

"Well, god, who'd 'ave thought it. You was my hero. You was a couple of years a'ead of me at school. Used to watch you play for the First XI after class. Wow!"

"I want to buy a 'ouse," I told him.

"Sure, great, what d'you have in mind? I've got a nice country 'ouse out near Borden, or there's a big place on Woodstock Road if you wanted somethin' nearer town."

"I wanna buy the house in the window, the one by the Rec."

"You don't mean the little terraced one?"

"Yeah, that's the one."

"Well, Mr. Steed."

"Billy."

"Billy, of course. Well, mate, it's in a bit of a state and it's a bit small."

"It's where I used to live as a kid," I told him.

"Oh, I see. A nostalgia thing. I get it. You'll probably want somethin' bigger too, right?"

"Maybe," I lied. It was what he wanted to hear after all. He thought I was a multi-millionaire ex-footballer looking for a country estate with a big front room for my big trophy cabinet and a big bedroom for my big-breasted trophy wife.

"Well, you wanna see the 'ouse by the park? I've got the keys. It's bin empty for a while. Seein' inside might put you off," he laughed.

"Let's go," I told him. I knew the house inside out and nothing was going to put me off buying it.

It was strange entering that house again. I'd remembered it as being small, but not quite as small as it was now. The front room still had the same fireplace, then there was the cramped little kitchen and dining area, the back door out to the overgrown garden. Upstairs were the two bedrooms and the little bathroom. I stayed for a while in the doorway of what had once been my room and remembered how it used to look with Christine sleeping on the bed waiting for me.

"Still wanna buy it?" asked the Estate Agent interrupting my daydreaming.

"Oh yes," I told him.

"If you're sure."

We got into his car to head back to the office and he suddenly produced another set of keys to show me.

"These are for the 'ouse out at Borden, it's really spectacular. What about if I show you now?"

"Sure, why not? I ain't got nothin' betta to do." He started the car happily and drove us out of town. The house was a small mansion with a wide driveway and beautiful lawns out amongst the cherry orchards. We walked through the big echoing rooms and I knew it wasn't for me. I could just imagine myself going crazy there alone in so much emptiness.

I was accustomed to the confined space of a cheap hotel room or even my prison cell. I couldn't live somewhere like this, not on my own.

On the way back into town, we stopped briefly on Woodstock Road to admire the front of the other house he thought I should be interested in, although he didn't have the keys and would have to ring the owner to arrange a viewing. I agreed that I might take a look on another occasion and we went back to town.

And so I finally took the big step of looking to own a house. The agent promised me he'd get me the best possible deal, he said that the owner's were desperate to sell having already moved somewhere bigger. I left it in his capable hands and gave him my mobile number. Then I went to the Red Lion for lunch, it had been an exhausting morning.

The next morning, to my surprise, Christine rang, the bloody mobile phone making me jump out of my skin as I lay on the bed reading a John Grisham. We arranged to meet later in the coffee shop in the Forum. I couldn't wait to tell her that I'd put in an offer for the house, the place that held so many memories for both of us.

Christine was pleased as punch when I told her my news, she said she had been worried that I might spend the rest of my life living in a hotel room. I didn't tell her that I wanted her to live there. I just told her that it would take a while for the deal to go through, although there was no chain, and that then I planned to redecorate. Perhaps an extension might be a good idea. If the house was extended out into the back garden we could have a bigger kitchen or a proper dining room and upstairs another bedroom or maybe two. I didn't tell any of this to Christine, it was just me getting ahead of myself, but I really liked the idea of her being happy there with her family.

We had a coffee and talked a bit and sat in silence a lot, but that didn't bother us, it never had done. When there was nothing to say, we were happy to say nothing. Of course there was something still left unsaid between us, I sensed that, but it was something for her to say, not me. Had she called for us to meet so that she could finally get off her chest whatever secret she was keeping from me? It was a secret that she had kept for over twenty years. If she had meant to tell me that morning then she chickened out, although she didn't seem distracted or worried or anything.

When both our coffee and our conversation had long run dry, we left and I walked with her to her car which was at the top of the multi-storey.

"Can we do this again?" I asked.

"Sure," she said with a smile.

"What, once a week?"

"Yeah, okay."

"'Ow 'bout twice?" I begged, pushing my luck perhaps.

"Twice? Okay then."

"So, Tuesdays and Thursdays at eleven, just like today?"

"If you like."

"And Saturday nights I take you out."

"I dunno. We can talk 'bout that on Thursday."

"Okay then," I agreed. She hadn't said no and she hadn't said maybe, which in my profound understanding of Christine was as good as a yes. I wanted to kiss her again. Why did I always want to kiss her?

"See ya Thursday," she said and she got into her car and drove slowly away. I stood there like an idiot watching her leave. Why did she always do that to me? Why did she always make me want to kiss her? It had always been that way when we were teenagers. Every time I had seen her, I'd wanted to spend all our time together kissing. Sometimes, I tried to force myself to wait an hour before allowing myself to kiss her, but I'd never got beyond five minutes. I worried that she might not want so much attention, although she never protested. Still, I worried about that. I worried about a lot of things. Most of all I worried about losing Christine. Maybe it was my worrying so much that had caused her to leave me. Maybe there was no big secret for her to tell, maybe she just got fed up with my worrying. All these years I'd thought that perhaps she had met someone else, or perhaps she had gotten bored of me, but now I had a new reason for her having left me. I don't remember ever having told her that I worried about losing her, but maybe women just sensed those sorts of things.

And so I had coffee twice a week to add to my list of routines, and maybe dinner on Saturday nights too. My simple life after prison was beginning to get more and more complicated. I had a mobile phone, the promise of owning a house and of course I had Christine back in my life.

EIGHT

Our second league game was away against Lydd Town. For those of you who aren't perhaps as familiar with lower league football as you should be, or with Kentish geography for that matter, that's down on Romney Marsh near Dungeness, just on the Kent/Sussex border. It was a bit of a journey for us, down the M20 in Clive's new minibus towards Folkestone, and when we arrived, we found a gale blowing in off the sea. I knew from then on that it was never going to be a pretty game.

I called for a big effort from my lads. I told them it was going to be a game of two very distinct halves of football. I made them understand that when we were playing against the wind it was imperative to keep the ball on the deck, short hard passes, especially out of defence. Anything up in the air would just come straight back at us. And waste time. Against the wind waste time. Every time the ball was out of play walk to get it, never run. Goal kicks, throw ins, take all the time you can. Then, with the wind, be careful to under hit everything, otherwise the ball would just race away down the pitch, and keep the ball in play as much as possible.

Clive Junior won the toss and we started against the wind as I'd suggested to him. The opposition swarmed all over us with the gale behind them and we were pushed back in our own half for long periods. I dropped Cheesy back into midfield and just left Charlie Chalk alone up front for most of the time. We were two goals down at half time. I told the lads not to worry, that things were going to be very different after the break. And so it proved. We got the two goals back fairly quickly and pressed forward relentlessly looking for our first win. But it wasn't to be, their keeper had an inspired afternoon and when Charlie Chalk headed against the bar in the last minute, we had to settle for a draw. Still, it was our first league point, but more importantly we had played well. I felt we were very close to being able to at last win a match. I hoped the players felt it too.

That night I got fish and chips for everyone at Christine's house and then, when she'd put Little Billy to bed, we walked into town for a drink at the Bull. We sat in the window and watched the wind blow crisp packets up and down the High Street in front of Woolworths.

"'Ow's the 'ouse deal comin' along?" she asked.

"My offer was accepted. Now it's up to the lawyers to do their thing. Estate agent reckons six to eight weeks if everythin' goes smoothly. There ain't no chain."

"'Ave you got your mortgage sorted out?"

"Mortgage?"

"Yeah, y'know. 'Ave you spoken to the bank? I mean, I don't wanna put a downer on it or nothin', but you ain't got any income. You might well find that nobody'll lend you the money," she explained. I burst out laughing.

"God Christine, you ain't got a clue, 'ave you?"

"Ain't got a clue 'bout wot?" she wanted to know, starting to sound annoyed.

"What d'you think professional footballers get paid?" I asked.

"I dunno," she replied, "you ain't a professional footballer no more and you ain't bin for a long time."

"I used to earn more in a week than most people earn in ten years, and that's just basic salary. Add on win bonuses and endorsements and it probably doubled again. You remember those beer adverts I did?"

"Yeah, some Spanish beer weren't it?"

"Yeah, they paid me a fortune."

"My second husband stopped drinking it after you started appearing in the adverts."

"'Is loss, it's a great beer."

"What you're sayin' then is you're rich?"

"Let's just say I could buy all the 'ouses 'round the park and still 'ave plen'y left over. When I went into prison, my accountant invested everythin' and now I'm worth ten times what I was when I wen' in."

"You're shitting me!"

"It's true Chris. The estate agent showed me a million pound mansion out near Borden, I could buy that no problem."

"So why on earth d'you wanna buy your old 'ouse?"

"I want you to 'ave it," I told her. I hadn't meant to, it just slipped out.

"What?"

"I want you to 'ave it. I wan' you to live there wiv your kids," I tried to explain.

83

"Yeah? An' what d'you want in return?"

"What d'you mean?"

"You can't buy me Billy Steed," she snapped and jumped to her feet and stormed out of the pub. I just stayed there, open-mouthed in shock. I sat for a while trying to work out why she should be so offended, but I couldn't figure it out. Of course I should just have kept my big mouth shut. Maybe she'd calm down and give me a call the next day to say that everything was all right, maybe there'd just be another twenty years of silence.

Sunday, she didn't call. On Tuesday morning I was sat in the coffee shop waiting for her by half past ten. At five past eleven I left because I knew she wasn't going to show up. On the Thursday I did it again and again she didn't come. She was killing me. Of course I could have rung her to apologise, but I wasn't sure exactly what I'd done wrong. Better to let things lie for a bit longer I decided. I'd always been a bit of a coward with women.

I harboured the forlorn hope that come Saturday, Little Billy would pester her about coming over to the Island to watch the match, and she would crumble under the pressure. It poured with rain all Saturday morning and no one turned up. The only person there was the member of the Stevedore's Club who had been sent to take entry money, standing lost and alone under a huge golf umbrella by the gate. When the match kicked off, he gave up and went home, leaving a little pile of soggy team sheets in the bin by the gate.

It was a terrible shame that there was no one there to witness my first victory as a manager. No TV cameras, not even a photographer. I sat huddled up to Clive in the dugout, the rain thudding down like incessant drumming upon the metal roof, and watched in awe as my team totally outplayed the opposition and ran out comfortable 3-0 winners. It wasn't just any opposition either, it was Oakwood, who had won their first two games and were firm favourites to win the league. We certainly gave them something to think about for the long season ahead.

When the final whistle blew, Bob hurried from his beautifully warm BMW in the car park, from which comfort he had watched the match, to congratulate me. He hugged me as if I'd just delivered my first FA Cup or something.

"We was fantastic," he enthused.

"We was," I agreed. "And we're gonna get even better."

"Wow Boss, the formation really worked well today," said Ginger who looked like a drowned brown rat from so many muddy tackles. He offered me his hand to shake, but I ignored him and hugged him to me, mud and all.

"You were awesome out there," I told him, and it was true. The world's most unlikely-looking footballer had been a monster. I couldn't remember a single occasion when anyone had got past him.

The changing room was a glorious cacophony of noise as only a winner's changing room can be. I just felt so relieved for this team which had gone the whole of the previous season without a single victory, and of course, I was so relieved for myself. I felt like a huge weight had been lifted from my shoulders.

In the bar afterwards, we all sat together and drank a well-earned beer that Bob, the Chairman, decided to buy. We toasted our club and promised ourselves plenty more victories.

Back at the hotel in the evening, as I was having dinner alone, my mobile phone rang. My heart jumped as I thought that it might be Christine asking me why the fuck I hadn't turned up to take her out as it was Saturday night, but it wasn't her. It was the sports reporter for the local paper. He apologised for not having been at the game, he said he had been at Central Park in Sittingbourne instead, and he asked me for the result. I told him about our win and described the match for him so that he could write it up. He promised to come back to see us as soon as he could.

Later that night, when the hotel bar finally emptied, I staggered up the stairs to my room and spent an hour sitting on my bed staring at my mobile. Of course I wasn't expecting it to ring, I was just wondering whether or not to call Christine. Sometime around 1am, I decided it was too late and reluctantly went to sleep. It should have been a happy moment for me, but I'd actually never felt so alone. With the light off and the distant sound of snoring from another room, it was just like being back in prison.

I kept to my routine of going to the coffee shop on Tuesdays and Thursdays, routines were good for me, even if not seeing Christine made me feel bad. Just as seeing our bench every morning in the park when I was jogging made me feel bad. Just as every time my bloody mobile rang and it wasn't her I felt bad. I really wanted to throw the bloody thing away, but it was my only faint lifeline to Christine and so I kept it close by at all times and checked it regularly just in case I hadn't heard it ring or something. I charged the battery lovingly every three or four nights and willed it to somehow tell her mobile to call.

Our first league victory was followed by another and then another, and soon we were on a run of nine straight wins by the end of November. We were seven points clear of Oakwood at the top of the table and playing better with each game. We had stopped training at the prison after the clocks went back, and now we met on Wednesday nights at the sports centre in Sheerness for some indoor five-a-side paid for by a very happy chairman.

At the beginning of December, I got a phone call from Charlie Chalk asking me to go to his parole hearing and put in a good word for him. I told him that I didn't think that a good word from an ex-con was going to do him much good, but he really seemed to want me to be there. And so I went with Bob and we both said nice things about the lad, and to my surprise he was given a release date of just before Christmas. He was understandably overjoyed and broke down into tears when he heard the news. He hugged Bob and I for ages and cried his heart out and then made us promise that we wouldn't say a word to the rest of the team about his tears. We promised. He planned to move in with Cheesy and Ginger who had found an old couch for him to use in their squat in Queenborough. He promised himself that he would never go back to prison. I'd promised myself that as well, and so far so good.

My lawyer rang me the following day to say that we were ready to exchange contracts on the house, and that as long as there were no last minute hiccups I should be able to move in for Christmas. Christmas? I didn't give a fuck about Christmas, why should I? Then I had the brilliant idea of letting Charlie, Cheesy and Ginger move into my house. They were nice lads who just hadn't had a chance at a life and I knew that without a bit of help they would all be in and out of prison, possibly for the rest of their lives. Somewhere half decent for them to live with running water and electricity and central heating might really make a difference.

I decided to pay a visit to the pie factory where my dad had worked as I knew they were always looking for staff. I was surprised to find the same old manager there from my father's day. He'd been a big fan of mine throughout the years he said. I begged him to give three young lads the chance of a job at the factory and he agreed that I could bring them to meet him. I arranged for Cheesy and Ginger to come over to Sittingbourne on the train the next day and Charlie Chalk could start in the New Year.

After their interview and a brief tour of the factory, I walked them across the park and stopped them in front of my childhood home.

"This is where you're gonna live," I told them.

"What do y'mean Boss?" asked Ginger.

"It's my 'ouse. You guys are gonna rent it. I won't charge you much, just look after it. It's ain't a squat and it's where I grew up."

"You serious?" gasped Cheesy.

"Yeah," I said, "I bought it to give to someone, but that didn't work out so I'd like you guys to 'ave it."

"Wow!" said Ginger, "thanks Boss."

"Don't let me down boys and work 'ard at the factory – my dad worked there most of 'is life."

"We won't let you down Boss," said Cheesy with a serious face I'd never seen him use before.

NINE

Our last league game before Christmas was at home to Kennington who were bottom of the league. It was a cold day, but not too bad, it wasn't raining or windy or anything. Ginger picked me up at the hotel and I sat in the front of his wreck of a car and tried to act unafraid. Chalk and Cheese slept in the back or at least they pretended to, maybe they were scared too. I was surprised when we arrived at the Stevedore's Ground to find Christine's dad sitting in his car with Little Billy. I went over to say hello.

"Looking well," I said to Christine's dad, and he was too.

"I feel great. Decided it was time to start driving again, so 'ere we are."

Little Billy gave me a huge smile and held up his football. We kicked around for a bit and then I went to give my team talk. It was easy enough, just play the way we always play. Don't do anything different and don't drop the level of effort just because they're the bottom club. When we went out for the kickoff, I saw that no one else had turned up to watch, last Saturday shopping before Christmas and all that, so I told Christine's dad to sit in the dugout with Clive, whilst Little Billy and I stood at the side and shouted encouragement at the players.

It was a stroll in the park, a comfortable 5-0 victory to keep our winning streak going. After a round of drinks in the bar, Christine's dad offered me a lift back to Sittingbourne and, of course, I gratefully accepted rather than risk my life once more in Ginger's no brakes wreck. When we stopped outside the Conistan Christine's dad leaned across towards me as if he were going to impart some top secret information.

"We'd like you to come for Christmas dinner," he said rather formally.

"That's nice of you," I told him, "but I wouldn't wanna come if it ain't al'right wiv Christine."

"It's al'right wiv Christine," he said. "Listen, I dunno what's goin' on 'tween you two, and it ain't none of my business, but she's been in a permanent bad mood lately. I think you should come for Christmas an' sort things out with 'er. It's obvious you both wanna be together."

"I won't come 'less she asks me," I said.

"You're as pig-headed as she is," he laughed.

"Tell 'er I'll be at the coffee shop on Tuesday if she wants to invite me 'erself."

"Okay, I'll tell 'er. What time?"

"She knows."

And so Tuesday morning I went to the coffee shop as usual, only this time I found Christine there waiting for me.

"Al'right," I said as I sat down across the table from her.

"Al'right," she replied. "How's things?"

"Good, I guess."

"Dad told me your team keeps winning."

"Yeah."

"Sorry I didn't come over the other day, last minute Christmas shopping, y'know."

"Sure."

"Okay John. What d'you want me to say? Sorry?"

"That'd be nice."

"So, sorry, okay? Does that make you 'appy?"

"I weren't trying to buy ya Christine. I wanted you to 'ave the 'ouse for you and your kids. I didn't buy it to live in myself, I still live at the 'otel, I kind of like it there. I never in a million years thought we'd move in together."

"No?"

"No." She looked into my eyes to see if I was telling the truth. I knew Christine could read me like a book, but at that moment I didn't give a shit that she knew I was lying.

"So, you gonna come for Christmas dinner? Mum would love to 'ave ya."

"No, I ain't."

"Why?" she asked a look of shock on her face.

"'Cause I ain't playin' games no more."

"What d'you mean?"

"I mean it's truth time."

"Truth 'bout what?"

"You know about what."

89

The waitress brought my usual coffee and my usual jam doughnut over. Routines are good, they're all I have. I took a big bite of doughnut and looked expectantly at Christine. If she didn't finally open up then I was leaving. Fuck Christmas dinner, fuck her, but I was leaving with a mouthful of doughnut. I raised my eyebrows to let her know I was ready. She gave a big sigh.

"Your dad told me to finish wiv ya," she whispered.

"My dad?"

"Yeah. It was that Saturday. I got up early to make us a picnic. It was your first Saturday without a match. I thought we could cycle out to Ship On Shore. Your dad rang me."

"Why'd my dad ring you?"

"'E said 'e'd 'ad a phone call from Gilling'am and they wanted to sign you. 'E reckoned you wouldn't go as long as we was together. 'E asked me to finish with you so that you'd accept the offer."

"An' you did."

"I knew you wanted to be a footballer. I didn't wanna stand in your way. Besides, your dad said it'd only need to be for a few weeks, just so you'd sign an' get your O Levels out of the way. Then 'e said we could get back together..."

"Don't believe ya Christine," I said.

"It's true John. I swear."

"An' what 'appened to the gettin' back together part?"

"I guess you was too angry with me."

"Me?"

"Well, I called your dad an' 'e told me you 'ad moved to Rain'am to live, so I asked 'im for your phone number. 'E said not to worry that 'e'd get ya to call me. You never called."

"My dad never told me. 'E just said 'e'd seen you in town one day and you was wiv someone else."

"Well, that ain't true. I weren't wiv no one for a long time."

"So, my dad split us up."

"Looks that way. Why'd 'e do that? I thought 'e liked me."

"'E was obsessed with me becoming a professional. 'E wanted it more than I did. I guess 'e was sure I wouldn't sign for Gilling'am wiv you around."

"Then 'e did the right thing."

"What d'you mean?"

"I wouldn't 'ave wanted you to miss out on your career 'cause of me."

"That's all well and good, and hats off to you and my dad, but y'got it all wrong."

"What d'you mean?"

"I mean, I'd rather 'ave stayed at Sheppey United, I'd rather 'ave stayed in Sittin'bourne and I'd rather 'ave kept you as my girlfriend."

"Then I'm sorry," said Christine and she took my hand. I could see a tear forming in the corner of her eye.

"Then let's not waste any more time," I told her.

"You're right," she agreed. I got up from my seat and went to her and held her in my arms. It felt so right, and all the hurt of all those years just seemed to melt away. We kissed. It was a slightly doughnut-flavoured kiss, but it was a wonderful one. Lord knows I'd waited so long for it.

"So, you'll come to Christmas dinner then?" whispered Christine when we finally broke our kiss.

"Okay, but I want you to 'elp me get presents for everyone, I ain't turning up empty-'anded. Little Billy needs an Ars'nal shirt, but the rest I ain't got a clue. I know what to get you though."

"What?"

"Come on, I ain't gonna tell ya"

And so Christine and I went shopping. Then we had lunch at the Red Lion and then we separated and she headed back to her parent's house and I went to see my favourite estate agent.

"Billy Steed, welcome back mate," he gushed when I entered the office. "'Ow's the 'ouse by the park?"

"It's fine," I reassured him. "I wanted to know if you still 'ad that 'ouse near Borden what you showed me."

"I knew you liked it, I could tell."

"Well, to be 'onest it wasn't right for me at the time, but it's just what I need now."

We agreed on what would be a reasonable offer seeing as the house had been up for sale for quite a time in a falling market, and I took a copy of the details of the house with a few photographs to put in Christine's

Christmas card. I just knew she would love it. I just knew we were going to be happy there.

I struggled back to the hotel laden down with bags full of presents. I had remembered to buy some wrapping paper, but I had never wrapped a present in my life. I just hoped that my favourite receptionist would be on duty sometime in the next 24 hours to give me a hand. When I reached the hotel I was glad to see her at the desk.

"Mr. Steed," she called out when she saw me, "I've got a message for you." I walked over to the desk, put my bags down on the floor and took the piece of paper she held out to me. It simply said that Gillingham Football Club had rung and there was a number to call back. I wondered what on earth Gillingham could possibly want with me. I asked the receptionist if she could give me a hand wrapping presents a bit later and she agreed, then I struggled up the stairs to the attic.

I threw everything on the bed, took out my mobile and rang the number on the message form. I told the girl who answered who I was and was surprised when she told me she was putting me through to the Chairman. I heard the ring of a distant extension.

"Billy Steed, hello," said the Gills' Chairman when he came on the line. "I wanted to be the first to congratulate you."

"For what?" I asked feeling suddenly very confused.

"You mean you 'aven't 'eard?"

"'eard what?"

"My god man, where 'ave you bin all day?"

"Shoppin'."

"Shoppin'? Then you ain't 'eard that the newspaper what broke the story that got you sent to prison has been closed down by the police. They've seized all their files."

"What's that gotta do wiv me?"

"The police said the newspaper was payin' people to lie 'bout certain stories they wrote. One of 'em was yours', according to Sky News."

"What does that mean?"

"Well, the investigation is still underway, but it could mean you'll be given a pardon, at least that's what they're saying on TV."

"God!" I said. "I can't believe it. Thanks for tellin' me, I'll put the news on."

"Billy, listen, there's one more thing I wanted to say."
"Yeah?"
"I expect you know we sacked our manager last week."
"Sure I 'eard," I lied.
"Well, I was wonderin' if you'd be int'rested in the job?"
"Me?"
"Yeah, we couldn't think of anyone more qualified to save the club from relegation than an ex-England captain. And seein' as you used to play for us, we know the fans'll get behind you straight away."
"Jesus! This is all a bit of a shock to the system."
"Well, 'ow about you come an' watch the game at Priestfield on Boxing Day as my guest and we talk things over? Does that sound al'right?"
"Sounds great."
"I'll send someone from the club to pick you up."

When I got off the phone I grabbed the remote and put the TV onto Sky News. Sure enough, at the bottom of the screen on the rolling tickertape was the headline story of the day as breaking news. My god it could really be true. I sat on the bed shaking, unable to believe what a day I was having. It looked as if I just might get my life back, the life I should have had. My mobile rang. It was Christine.

"Oh John, 'ave you 'eard?"
"Yeah, I've got the news on now."
"Ain't it wonderful?"
"It's amazing."
"It's gonna be a fantastic Christmas after all," she said.
"It's gonna be the best Christmas ever," I assured her.

APPROACHING SILENCE

ONE

Jim Sharp's eyes fluttered open. He blinked rapidly as he tried to get a focus on his surroundings. Above him was a ceiling so white that it hurt his eyes to look at it, just as if it were snow on a sunny day. It was all he could see. Was he in some new brilliant white place? Was this heaven? He lay on his back, the white snow ceiling above him. He dared not move his head to one side, since it felt like it might split open if he did so. Had someone beaten him over the head with a rock? He couldn't remember. He couldn't remember anything.

He heard a door open somewhere close at his right hand side, but he still couldn't bring himself to move his head.

"You're alive then?" came an unfamiliar female voice. A young woman dressed in a nurse's uniform flitted into view at the bottom of the bed in which he was lying. She picked up a clipboard and began to write something. Jim looked down through the bottom of his eyes towards the end of the bed. She was young and pretty and he had always had a thing for a nurse's uniform. Maybe this place was indeed heaven. But then maybe it was a brothel. Yes, that was it. He had got pissed and fallen asleep in a bloody brothel. That was why his head hurt so much. What he had was a really bad hangover. Shit, if he'd spent the whole bloody night in a brothel god only knew what his bill was going to come to. He tried to raise himself up, but a strong pain in his head made him give up with a loud groan.

"Try not to move," said the young woman. That was easy for her to say, she probably charged by the hour. Jim tried to speak, to at least ask where he was, but his throat was so sore that no words would come out. His head had now become a tunnel with an express train pounding through it. This couldn't be heaven, he wouldn't feel this bad in heaven. He tried to swallow but couldn't bear the pain.

"I'll get you some water shall I?" he heard the nurse say. Thank Christ for that. She gingerly cradled Jim's head and pressed a cool glass to his lips. He took a small sip of water and held it in his mouth letting the moisture slowly revive his swollen tongue. The glass came again to his lips and he took a bigger gulp and swallowed it instantly, the pain was sharp and stabbing, like shards of broken glass all the way down his throat.

"Feel any better?" asked the woman.

"Feel like shit," mumbled Jim. The nurse just laughed. "Where am I?"

"South Side Hospital Mr. Sharp."

"Hospital? You really are a nurse then?"

"Of course I'm a nurse, what did you think I was?"

Jim didn't answer, he just closed his eyes and tried to remember what might have brought him to a hospital.

"Did I have a stroke? Heart attack?"

"Don't be silly Mr. Sharp. You fell down drunk in the street and bashed your head on the curb."

"Drunk?"

"Yep. Doctor said you were lucky not to get alcohol poisoning. How much did you have?"

"Don't remember, couple of whiskies maybe."

"A couple?" The nurse laughed. She had a nice laugh, but it made Jim's head hurt even more. "Couple of bottles more like. You could've died." She laughed again. Jim's head throbbed with pain once more. Why did she have to keep laughing? What was there to laugh at?

"What time is it?"

"Eleven. I should try and rest a bit. The press are waiting to speak to you. You don't want to talk to them yet I take it?"

"Fuck no. I need to phone my agent."

"You mean Mr. Brown?"

"Yeah, Blimey Brown. Worst agent a man could have."

"I don't suppose you're the world's best client, are you Mr. Sharp?"

Jim snorted in disgust, but didn't bother to argue with her. If the truth were told, Blimey Brown was the only agent in the world who would have had anything to do with Jim Sharp. They went back a long way. Blimey had known Jim almost from the start, way back when they were both young and enthusiastic and talented. Blimey had gone onto ever greater things, his list of clients was the most impressive in London. He had branched out from his sporting roots, and he now had pop stars, actors and actresses, TV personalities, writers and even politicians on his books. Probably, most of them figured that if he could make money for

Jim Sharp then he could make a veritable fortune for them. They couldn't know that Blimey kept faith in Jim just for old time's sake. Sure he still took his ten percent, but as he often reminded Jim, ten percent of peanuts was just peanuts.

It had been Blimey who had negotiated Jim's latest and no doubt his last contract. When it appeared no one would touch the thirty-three year old drunken has been, Blimey had got him a new deal, a two year deal at that. It was perhaps the greatest piece of contract negotiation in sporting history. There was no doubt about it; Blimey Brown was a class act.

Jim was awoken a couple of hours later by a commotion from the corridor outside his room. There was an army of different voices firing off a barrage of questions, and booming right back, calm and unruffled, came the voice of Blimey Brown, repeating, time and again, as patiently as he could, the phrase "no comment!"

There was a scuffle immediately outside Jim's door and then Blimey and the nurse burst in, slamming the door quickly behind them so that no pictures could be taken. There were a few last shouted comments from outside, and then quiet.

Jim, who was feeling a little bit better after his recent sleep, sat up to look at his agent.

"Blimey!" said Blimey Brown. "You look like shit, Razor."

"Feel like shit," his client informed him.

"What's the official version as far as his health is concerned nurse?" asked Blimey.

"He's kinda fucked up," replied the nurse.

"Kinda fucked up? Is that what you expect me to tell the press?"

"No, you could always tell them the truth He was pissed, fell over in the street and banged his head. He's got a bad concussion and a nasty hangover."

"She's right about the hangover," put in Razor.

"You can shut up," snapped Blimey.

"Only trying to help."

"I don't want your help, you've gone and shot yourself in the foot again. God knows how I'm gonna get you out of this one."

"Aren't you going to tell the press the truth then?" asked the nurse with a smile.

"Good god no!" snorted Blimey Brown almost choking on the mention of the word truth. It wasn't a word he was too familiar with, especially not where dealings with the press were concerned. His oldest client and oldest friend, Jim 'Razor' Sharp, was in the shit again and the truth was the very last thing they wanted the press to get a hold of.

Blimey paced around the room, his left hand over his mouth, desperately trying to think of something. At last he had a flash of inspiration.

"Blimey! I've got it," he shouted triumphantly.

"'Bout bloody time too," put in Razor, "I was beginning to think you were losing your touch."

"We'll tell the press you were out walking your dog."

"Don't have a dog."

"Don't interrupt me. We'll tell 'em you were out walking your dog and you came across some skinheads mugging an old lady. And you, the brave and fearless Razor Sharp of London Athletic, jumped right in, threw a couple of punches, chased the skinheads away and saved the old girl from certain death."

"Bravo," said Jim, a little too loudly for his hangover.

"Aren't you missing an old lady for this story?" asked the nurse.

"We'll just say she didn't want any publicity," decided Blimey Brown.

"Still don't have a dog," moaned Razor.

"Will you shut up about a fucking dog. We'll get you one as soon as you're up and about. A poodle or something."

"A poodle? Fuck off! A man who battles skinheads and rescues old ladies should have a huge great Doberman."

"Yeah, right. You get a Doberman and the first time you come home pissed late at night, having forgotten to feed it, the bastard thing'll rip you to shreds. Or worse still, you'll be taking it for a walk in the local park and it'll tear off a kid's arm. Not even I could make you look like a hero after that."

"Okay, I'll settle for a greyhound then, something sleek and athletic like myself."

The nurse burst out laughing.

"You'd have to walk miles and miles if you got a greyhound, the exercise would fucking kill you," laughed the agent.

"A greyhound could be just what I need to get fit for the new season," stated Jim, sounding unusually sincere.

"Fit? You? You haven't been fit since you were twenty-one back at United, before you went on the booze, before you started staying out all night, before you fucked up your career."

"Don't know why I keep you on. Who needs an agent like you?"

"You do. So, we go with the dog, the old lady and the three skinheads story then, right?"

"Five skinheads," said Razor.

"I think three's enough. Nurse, could you get him some mouthwash from somewhere. If the press get a nose full of the whiskey fumes from his mouth the story's up in smoke."

There was a knock at the door.

"It's me, Angie," came a high-pitched familiar female voice.

"Oh fuck! How the hell did she find out that I was here?" moaned Razor pulling his bed sheet up over his head.

"She called me just as I was leaving the office and asked where you were. She said she had something to tell you, something important. She came down to London yesterday, of course she didn't expect to have to come to visit you in hospital."

"Something important?" laughed Razor from beneath his sheet, "I bet someone's just told her I've dropped out of the Premiership and taken a pay cut. Now she's worried about payments for that brat of hers."

"He's your brat too Jim," said Angie who had let herself into the room.

"Yeah? We've only got your word for that. What's the little bastard's name anyway? I can't even remember." Razor pulled back the sheet.

"Mikey, say 'hi' to your dad," said Angie pushing forward a shy looking eight year old who was wearing a face that said it was about to burst into tears.

"Hi Jim," mumbled the boy, and then he retreated back behind his mother.

"That ain't the same kid you had before is it?"

"Of course he is, don't be stupid."

"Last time I saw him he was only half that size."

"Been a few years hasn't it. Some father you turned out to be."

"What d'you mean? I pay for the bloody kid don't I?"

"Only 'cause you know you'd end up in court again if you didn't."

"Let's call a truce for a bit shall we?" put in Blimey, who was already late for a meeting with a possible new client, a page three stunner at that, not the kind of lady he wanted to keep waiting any longer than was absolutely necessary. "Let's get the press off your back Jim and then you and Angie can argue for the rest of the day as far as I'm concerned."

"Shall I let them in?" asked the nurse. She handed Razor a small plastic cup of mouthwash that he knocked back in one go.

"You're not supposed to bloody drink it!" exploded Blimey, "you're just supposed to gargle it a bit and then spit it out."

"Now you tell me," said Razor giving a broken-toothed smile through his untidy beard. Blimey, temporarily dumbstruck, nodded towards the nurse, who dutifully opened the door for the press boys to come in.

As the small, but loud, group of reporters and photographers burst into Razor's hospital room, so they began a barrage of questions, one on top of the other, everyone shouting at once. No single question could have been understood and no answers were expected, it was just what the press had to be seen to do, at least by each other. Razor closed his eyes as cameras flashed in his face. Skilfully, Blimey manoeuvred Jim's eight year old son into the frame and photographers happily snapped away at this rare father and son opportunity. The boy bore no resemblance whatsoever to Jim, he was blonde, tall and thin, good-looking just like his mother, he was not dark, fat and ugly like his father. Razor had the face of a bad but determined boxer and the body of a steak and kidney pie salesman who liked to take his work home with him. Jim had always doubted that the boy was his. There had been rumours in the press back then that his wife was having an affair with some drugged-up rock star, but then there had been different stories every week about his supposed latest bit on the side. Back then he had only to talk to a girl at a club or at a party for her picture to get into the papers. The girls knew it too and many came looking for him just for that. There had even been a few kiss and tell birds who had bared their tits for page three and said they'd shagged in Jim's sports car or in some dodgy hotel. Razor was fairly sure it was all lies, although there were parts of his life that he just couldn't remember at all.

The year or so leading up to his divorce was just a blur, as was the year after come to that. He remembered the day of the divorce though, he hadn't had a drink for twenty-four hours in order to create a good impression on the judge, although he needn't have bothered as the old bastard stitched him up good and proper. As soon as he was out of court the United Physio drove him to the airport and they got a flight to Rome where, later that evening, in one of his last appearances in the United first team, Jim became the legendary Razor Sharp once again, leading the line and scoring a hat trick in a breath-taking performance. Two weeks later he was in court again on an assault charge after a fight outside a Manchester club. He didn't bother to stay sober for that hearing. The judge ordered him to serve three months although he was out in one, but it was the final nail in the coffin for his United career. That was when the bottom dropped out of his world.

Blimey held up his hands theatrically to bring some sort of order to the proceedings in the crowded hospital room.

"I have a short statement to make on behalf of my client, then Jim will answer a few questions, but keep it brief please gentlemen as he needs to rest."

There was a murmur of consent and a collective nodding of heads and then Blimey launched into his statement.

"Last night at approximately 11.45 p.m. my client, Jim Sharp, was out walking his dog in the local park when he came across an elderly lady being attacked by a gang of shaven-headed youths. With complete disregard for his own safety, Mr. Sharp rushed to the lady's defence and managed to scare the attackers off. Unfortunately, during the mêlée my client was hit on the back of the head by a baseball bat which is why he is now in hospital suffering from a severe concussion. Any questions anyone?"

"What's the name of the old lady?" asked one reporter.

"She doesn't want any publicity, so we've agreed not to release her name. She's at home with her family recovering from her terrifying ordeal, which would of course have been a lot worse were it not for my client's fortuitous arrival on the scene."

"How long will you be in hospital Jim?"

"Don't know," said Razor.

"He should be out in twenty-four hours," put in the nurse causing the reporters to take up their cameras and get a picture of her to brighten up an otherwise dull story.

"What dog have you got Razor?" was the next question. Jim could only think of a poodle and was just about to say that he couldn't remember what type of dog he had, when Blimey came to his rescue.

"It's a greyhound, Jim's been out running with it to help along his pre-season training. You'll have to forgive us now gentlemen, but he really does need to get some rest."

"One last question," put in a reporter from the Evening Standard whose paper would be the first to run the story, "who does your son support Razor?"

There was a silence as everyone waited for an answer. Razor looked at the boy, but the boy had his eyes down looking at the floor. He was blushing.

"Don't know," said Jim quietly, realising that he didn't know anything at all about the boy.

"Mikey supports whichever team his father is playing for," put in Blimey Brown.

"So his favourite team gets relegated every year then, poor kid," laughed the reporter who had asked the question.

"Right now he supports London Athletic and he's looking forward to seeing his dad bang in the goals to take them back to the Premiership. Well, that really is it everyone, thank you for your time and we wish you all a very good day."

The nurse helped Blimey Brown usher the press boys out of the room, and at last the damage limitation exercise was done.

"That went okay," said Razor.

"It was all a pack of lies and a complete crock of shit, as always, as far as anything to do with you is concerned," snapped Angie turning on him.

"Just be grateful that you're no longer a big enough star for the press boys to bother digging into this story. With any luck you'll get a few lines of praise in the back pages and then it'll all be forgotten," concluded Blimey, buttoning up his jacket and getting ready to leave.

"When do I get out of here nurse?" Razor wanted to know.

"The doctor said a minimum of twenty-four hours and then he'd come and see how you were doing," responded the nurse.

"Twenty-four hours? Are you bloody joking or what? I need to get out of here as soon as I can," moaned Razor.

"Oh yeah," agreed Blimey, "pre-season training starts tomorrow at ten, and he can't miss that."

"Fuck pre-season training," exploded Razor, "I need a bloody drink and I need one now. My head's gonna explode if I don't get a drink soon. Haven't you a got a hip flask or something? You're supposed to look after me."

"The last thing you need Mr. Sharp is a drink," put in the nurse.

"She's right Razor, you ought to lay off the booze for a few days," agreed the agent.

"Isn't there any booze here?" Razor asked the nurse putting on his little boy lost pleading for help voice.

"This is a hospital not a pub," she reminded him.

"Hospitals use alcohol don't they?" asked the patient.

"My god Jim, you're just so pathetic, listen to you begging for booze. It's always booze with you. Don't you see what a wreck you are? Can't you see what drink has done to you? To your career, to your body, to your life?" shouted Angie.

"You can shut up Angie, you liked a drink as much as I did back in the early days. We used to be out partying every night."

"I only used to go out to be with you, what was I supposed to do? Sit home and watch TV and wait for you to come in drunk, if you bothered to come back at all?"

"Sorry to interrupt this lovely family reunion, but I've got to make a move now," said Blimey Brown. He nodded goodbye to the nurse, ruffled Mikey's hair and left.

"I'm going to take a break and get a coffee," decided the nurse.

"Will you take Mikey with you please," begged Angie, "there's something important I've got to tell Jim."

"Okay, sure. Let's go get you a coke and a chocolate cookie shall we?" The boy said nothing but moved towards the nurse who took his hand and led him off down the corridor in the direction of the staff canteen.

103

"So, what is it you want to tell me Angie?" asked Razor.
"You're not going to like it Jim, not one bit."

TWO

Angie unbuttoned her jacket and laid it on the end of the bed. Razor found himself thinking that her blue jacket probably cost more money than his whole wardrobe put together, and the wardrobe itself come to that. Actually, he wasn't sure if he had a wardrobe or not, since he couldn't recall exactly where he was living at that particular moment. Maybe he had a rented flat, or the club had given him a house or maybe he was in a hotel for the time being. It was all too confusing and made his head hurt again. How many places had he had to call home since leaving United? He couldn't even begin to remember.

Angie came and sat on the bed next to him, a little too close for his liking, closer than they had been in years. He was suddenly glad that he wasn't hooked up to a life support machine because she would probably have taken the opportunity to pull the plug. Still, no one could blame her for that. She had certainly suffered at his hands; the beatings, the adultery, the lies and finally, despite all her efforts to help him get his life back on track he had abandoned her for an eighteen year old sex kitten, the same sex kitten that had ditched him within a couple of months of his divorce.

"Listen Angie, I'll do my best with the payments, okay? I know I'll be earning less from now on, but Christ, no Premiership outfit wanted me. I had to drop down a grade, I had no choice. Blimey got me a pretty good deal though all things considered. You know I don't waste time worrying about money. But there's no problem, as soon as my wages get paid into the bank they have instructions to forward your share."

"It's not about money. I wish it was. I haven't had any trouble getting the money for the last couple of years. If there's a problem I just ring Blimey and he sorts it out. He's a good bloke."

"Maybe you should have married him," said Razor.

"Maybe. I should've married anyone but you."

"Is that what this is about? You're getting married again. You didn't have to come here to tell me that. A phone call would have done."

"You have a phone?"

"No, don't think so."

"You must be the only person left in England who hasn't got a mobile phone, even Mikey's got one."

"No one would ever call me 'cept Blimey, and he'd just bug me about missing training or drinking on match days. Whatever the club complained to him about."

"Perhaps, if you'd listened to him occasionally you'd still be a good footballer."

"I still am a good footballer."

"Last time Mikey and I saw you on the tele you were so fat you couldn't even run. I don't think you touched the ball more than twice and they substituted you at half time."

"I didn't know you liked to watch football."

"I don't. Mikey wanted to see his dad, that's all."

"It's the job, it takes up all my time. You know how it is, training, playing, publicity shoots."

"Oh yes, I know how it is all right, pubs, pubs and more pubs. You can't fool me. I know you're a hopeless alcoholic."

"Alcoholic? Me?"

"You can't even admit it can you?"

"Okay, I like a drink, same as the next man, but I'm not an alcoholic."

"The next man? What next man?"

"Dunno, the pubs are full of blokes. You saying every man in England is an alcoholic?"

"No, not every man, just you." She put her hand over his bearded mouth before he could reply. "Listen Jim, believe it or not I didn't come here to argue. I didn't come here 'bout money and I'm not getting married again, besides, who in their right mind would want Jim Sharp's ex?"

"Why did you come?"

"There's no easy way to say this, so I'm just gonna come right out with it, okay?"

"Okay."

"I've got cancer."

"What?"

"I've got cancer. It started off as breast cancer, but it's spread and now there's nothing that can be done about it."

"Nothing? What about an operation? Don't they remove breasts with cancer and replace them with silicon ones?"

"Both of mine were silicon anyway, if you remember, but no, it's too late for operations."

"And chemotherapy, what about that?"

"Had it Jim. I've been in and out of hospital over the last year, there isn't anything I haven't tried, believe me. I lost half my body weight and all my hair during chemo, but it didn't cure me. There's nothing left but to wait to die."

"Surely there must be something left to try?"

"No, believe me, if there was something of a chance I'd take it, not for me, for Mikey. But, there's really nothing that can be done."

"How long you got? A couple of years?"

"No, the specialist reckons three months, maybe a bit more if I'm lucky."

"Three months? Jesus Christ, what can I say?"

"Nothing really. I'm not here for sympathy, I'm here about Mikey."

"What about him?"

"Unfortunately for him, you're the only family he's got."

"Me?"

"Yeah. You're his father, remember?"

"Of course I remember, but there must be someone else. What about your mother? He can go live with her, I'll send her all the money I can, I promise."

"My mum died last year. I think when she found out I had cancer it finished her off, she'd been very weak for a long time."

"Sorry 'bout that, although the old girl always hated my guts."

"D'you blame her?"

"No, guess not."

"She always said that the only good thing you ever did for me was Mikey. God she loved that boy, and he loved her too. He cried himself to sleep every night for months when she died. It's going to destroy him when I go too."

"So what do you want me to do?"

"I want you to be a father to your son."

"Me? A father? No way. I wouldn't know how to do it. And there's my lifestyle, all the travelling, the socialising, the publicity, how does a kid possibly fit into all that?"

"You'll have to make sacrifices Jim, like all parents do. Besides, you're thirty-three years old, it's time you finally grew up and took on some responsibility."

"I can't handle responsibility. How can I look after a kid when I can't even look after myself?"

"He needs a father figure in his life. He's been without one for too long."

"I never had a father and I turned out all right."

"Did you?" laughed Angie, "look at yourself. You're a fat, lazy, good for nothing alcoholic."

"I'm not an alcoholic. I'm a professional footballer. I used to play for Manchester United remember? I played for England, remember that?"

"Yeah, I remember, one game. What was it, ten minutes you lasted?"

"I got injured scoring a goal. I was out for eighteen months because I went in for that challenge with the goalkeeper and scored a goal that helped take us to the World Cup Finals in Italy. Without me England might never have reached the semi final. Without me Gazza would never have gotten on the plane."

"You're a has been Jim, face it. You've been living on that story for ten years. It's time you stopped feeling sorry for yourself about getting injured and got on with your life."

"What life?" sighed Razor, suddenly feeling exhausted.

"The one you could've had if it wasn't for the booze."

"I guess I was just lonely."

"Lonely! The great 'Razor' Sharp lonely? You had so many hangers-on you could've filled half of Old Trafford with them. And with all the bimbos you boys had in tow, you must've scored more times off the pitch than on it!"

"I had no real friends though."

"Don't try to give me some kind of hard luck story. You had it all. Fame, fortune, fast cars and even faster women. You loved it. You just loved walking into a pub or restaurant and being the centre of attention,

everyone asking you for your autograph, the blokes slapping you on the back, the women slipping you their phone numbers."
"Fame is a very fickle friend Angie, you know that as well as I do."
"Me?"
"Yeah, you were famous when I met you don't forget."
"I had ten minutes of fame, you've had ten years. Now you can't face the fact it's over."
"I heard your record on the radio the other day. They were reliving the eighties and it got played. They wondered what on earth ever happened to you."
"I met you, that's what happened. I gave up my career to be with you."
"Career? I don't think you could've made a career of singing. There was no way you could ever have followed up 'Do You Want To Touch My Sexy Body' it was just a one off."
"I should have made an album."
"No, you did the right thing to walk away from the limelight. I just wish I could've done it."
"What you? Walk away from football?"
"Yeah."
"Then do it. Do it now. Just quit. Just say you want to concentrate on bringing up your son. Tell the press that your famous popstar ex-wife, Angie Smith, is dying of cancer and you're quitting football to take over caring for your son."
"I can't just quit Angie. I've got a new contract."
"Quit Jim, save yourself the embarrassment of ever being filmed playing football again. Go out now and let people forget about the last few years and remember what you did at United."
"I can't quit."
"Well, you should. Where will you go next season? The Second Division, the Third? Is there a Fourth? I don't even know. How far down are you prepared to go? Don't you see that with every crap performance you put in you destroy a little bit more of your legend?"
"What else could I do? I don't know anything else."
"You could start by being a dad."
"I'd be a crap dad."

"Not if you quit the booze. You used to be an al'right guy until the booze took control of you."

"I can't quit. I've tried before. Booze is the only friend I've got."

"Booze isn't your friend Jim, it's your worst enemy. Look at yourself in the mirror sometime. No friend would do that to you."

"Okay, you've made your point. I'll try to give up."

"You can't do it alone. You need help. Call Alcoholics Anonymous or get the club to check you into an addiction centre or something."

"Okay, I'll sort it."

"I hope you do, for our son's sake. He needs you, he needs a father." She stood up and picked up her expensive jacket. "I'm going to find Mickey now. We'll come back this evening so that you can spend a bit of time with him, get to know him a bit."

"See you later. Sorry about the cancer thing. Sorry for everything, I guess."

"You see? You can still be a nice guy when you're not drunk!"

Jim was discharged from the hospital the following morning at nine after the doctor gave him the all clear as far as his head injury was concerned. He did tell the footballer that he ought to see his GP for a complete check over and that he should give up the booze for good. The nurse came in with Jim's clothes which she had taken home to wash since they stank of alcohol and cigarette smoke. It was the first time that his trousers had ever been ironed and they looked like new. She handed him his wallet which surprisingly contained a crisp new fifty pound note and a hotel key card, so at least he knew where he was staying.

"Thanks for everything nurse," said Razor when he was ready to leave.

"You're welcome Mr. Sharp. My dad's a big Athletic fan, he reckons you're the man to get them back into the Premier League. Don't let him done, okay?"

"Sure."

The nurse reached up on tiptoes and planted a kiss on Razor's big, ugly, bearded face.

"Look after yourself."

"I will." And he meant it too. He was going straight from the hospital to the hotel to get some kit, and then, ten o'clock sharp he would be there for training. This was a new start for him, the chance to turn over a new leaf. He would show the world that there were goals yet in Razor Sharp. He would lead London Athletic back to the Premiership and end his career with one final glory year back in the top division. He wasn't finished yet. There was still more of his legend to be written. He felt better than he had done in years, and for once he couldn't wait to get to training.

Jim paid the taxi driver with his new fifty pound note, pocketed the change and sprang up the steps to the entrance to his hotel.
"Morning Razor, good to see you back again," called out the receptionist as the footballer crossed the lobby to get to the lift. The hotel was unfamiliar, almost as if he had never been there before, and it took him a while to locate his room. Inside, the curtains were drawn and his fully-packed suitcase lay on the bed. Razor crossed the room and opened the curtains to allow some of the bright summer sunshine inside. It wasn't football weather, it was far too hot. In the good old days the league hadn't started until late August, but now it started earlier so that at the beginning of July they were in training, with pre-season friendlies coming soon afterwards. Razor had always loathed training sessions, even as a youth. It just seemed so pointless, all those hours of running, all that ball control and endless hours of shooting practice and, worse still, all those bullshit tactical meetings and planning sessions. Razor just let it all go in one ear and out of the other. He'd once fallen asleep in a United tactical briefing session and woken up a couple of hours later to find himself alone with just the Manager sitting waiting for him to wake up. The language used by the irate Manager when he saw Razor open his eyes took some digesting with a shroud of sleep hanging over him and a criminal hangover into the bargain, but even Razor understood that the Manager was not a happy man. He had been fined a week's wages, by no means the first time, and banished to the reserves for three games. When he returned to the first team he put the Manager firmly in his place by scoring four in a 6-0 drubbing of Ipswich, but Razor had learnt his lesson, he didn't fall asleep in a briefing session again at United, although whatever was said still went in one ear and out of the other.

111

Razor unzipped his suitcase and began to lay his untidy collection of belongings out on the bed. He came across a supermarket carrier bag and knew well enough what it contained. Opening it, he carefully removed a brilliant white England shirt, as new as the day it had been given to him, the number nine resplendent on the back, the three lions proud and fierce on the front. Having been injured and rushed to hospital, he had never had the opportunity to swap it with the opposition at the end of the game. So he had had it washed and ironed and had carried it in a plastic bag inside his suitcase ever since. The shirt was his own personal talisman. When he had moments of self doubt he would carefully extract it from its plastic bag and look at it. It would always give him inspiration and it was calming and fulfilling to know that he had once been considered good enough to play for his country. And yet, his one England cap had not just been the pinnacle of his career, it had also, to all intents and purposes, been the end. He had never been the same player or person since his horrific injury. Okay there had been specialists that had written him off and people in the press who had seemed to delight in reporting his latest setback on the long road to recovery, and he had proved them all wrong, all of them, everyone who had doubted him had been proved wrong, but he had never completely recovered. His blistering explosion of pace was gone, his ability to twist and turn out of trouble was no more, and more than anything his appetite for football had left him.

In the same plastic carrier, stuffed inside a brown paper bag, was his medal collection. During his time at United the club had won a host of trophies; three FA Cups, a European Cup Winners Cup, a League Cup and been back to back League Championships in 1992-93 and 1993-94. But, Jim hadn't appeared in any of the cup finals and so didn't own a winners medal. In 1985, he had been just an eighteen year old kid on the verge of breaking into the first team squad, with only five appearances and one goal behind him, so to be excluded from the final squad was not a surprise, but was nevertheless a huge disappointment. He remembered how the Manager had told him not to worry, that he had plenty of cup finals ahead of him, but it hadn't eased the pain. In 1990, United won the Cup again, but Jim was still eleven months away from fitness following his injury. And by the time United reached the final of 1994, the famous double-winning year, he was already promised to neighbours City and wasn't named in the squad. In the end, he didn't even receive a League Winner's medal, having made just nine substitute appearances in the double year. So, Jim's medal collection was not as large as people probably thought it was. He had missed the Cup Winners Cup Final and the League Cup Final through injury, so his only medals were the 1992-93 League Winners and two runners-up medals from 1987-88 and 1991-92. In the United side of the early nineties he had only been a bit-part player, but in the late eighties he had been the hero of Old Trafford, club top scorer for four consecutive seasons. He had felt invincible.

Jim didn't take the medals out to look at, he never did, they only caused him pain, and he quickly stuffed his England shirt back into the carrier on top of them. He stripped off his clothes and took a quick shower to wash the smell of the hospital from his body, and afterwards he checked out his reflection in the misty bathroom mirror. Angie was right, he looked like shit. His untidy beard was flecked with grey, his long hair, even recently washed, seemed lank and greasy and sported the same grey highlights as his beard. His skin was pale and unhealthy-looking, there were bags under his eyes and wrinkles across his forehead that he hadn't even noticed growing. Looking down past the greying hair of his chest he saw his gut sticking out obscenely. What the hell had happened to his body?

"You gotta do something Razor old boy," he said to his reflection, "this is your last chance. Don't blow it." He dressed quickly in an old tracksuit and rang reception to call him a taxi. It was while he was waiting for the taxi, sitting on his bed, that his eyes fell upon the minibar in the corner of the room. The fact that he hadn't headed straight for it on entering the room was no small victory for him, but, sitting there with nothing to do, the minibar seemed to be calling out to him. They shouldn't put minibars in hotel rooms that might be occupied by someone like himself who had a bit of a drink problem. He stood up and walked across the room and stood looking down at the dreaded minibar.

THREE

Jim found himself bending slightly, his body reacting as if of its own volition, his hand reaching down towards the chrome handle of the minibar. He could almost hear the clink of glass as he opened it, almost see those beautiful little whisky bottles winking at him. If he just had one quick drink it couldn't do any harm, surely? It would steady his nerves and relax him for training, yeah, just one drink would be a good thing.

The phone rang. He stood frozen for several seconds, his hand almost touching the handle of the minibar, and then, with a superhuman effort, he tore himself away and went to pick up the phone. His taxi was waiting. He hurriedly left the room without looking at the minibar, his heavy kit bag slung over his shoulder.

London Athletic's training facilities turned out to be rented rather than their own, but Razor didn't care. Training facilities had never been high on his list of priorities when choosing a club, and besides, this time he had had no choice at all. It was Blimey Brown who had got him this deal and Blimey had told him that it was all that was going. Jim had accepted it without even speaking to anyone from the club, except the doctor who had given him his medical. Blimey had convinced the doctor that his client would lose a few stone, control his diet and start to do regular exercise and the doctor had reluctantly let him pass. If the truth were known, London Athletic were in a bad way financially, and a free agent like Jim Sharp, whose contract with Nottingham Forest had not been renewed following their relegation, was the only sort of player they could hope to bring in. The playing squad had been decimated following the club's surprise last day of the season relegation, as its superstar players had desperately sought other Premiership clubs to take them on. It was like rats fleeing a sinking ship. Athletic of course let them go cheap since the wage bill had to be cut back to the bone if the club was going to survive in the Nationwide League. Jim's experience would be a valuable asset to the new-look squad if they were to avoid a second, catastrophic, relegation and besides, Razor was cheap. Blimey hadn't bothered at all about haggling for more salary than was originally on offer, he was just glad to get Jim off his back for another two years. Razor didn't care about money anyway, he never had done, as long as he had enough to fuel his drinking habit he was happy.

Blimey had forgotten to mention during negotiations that the five clubs Jim had played for since leaving United had all been relegated, four of them in his one and only year on their books. City had been the only club where he had played for more than a single season, but they were relegated in his second year and were glad to accept an offer from newly-promoted Sunderland to take their troublesome star striker off their hands.

Sunderland hadn't survived their first season back in the top flight and sold Jim to Barnsley who were also relegated at the first attempt. This time he was passed on to Forest. It was Blimey's wonder talents that had prolonged Jim's top flight career far longer than should have been possible. It was Blimey who had invented the relegation get out clause, and his oldest client who had made the best use of it. But his Forest deal had been for just one season and so he had been able to sign for London Athletic as a free agent.

Blimey didn't expect Razor to last more than a few months at Athletic, but at least he would be on hand to negotiate a reasonable payoff for his friend when the time came. Maybe he could persuade Jim to open a sports shop or something and finally get him off his books. Razor brought in the least money of any of Blimey's clients by far and took up as much of his time as all the rest put together. But they were friends from way back when they had both started with nothing, and that meant a lot to Blimey, even though Jim was now a complete pain in the arse to deal with.

London Athletic's new manager was a former Manchester United player who had been in the same team as Razor back in the late eighties and therefore remembered what Jim had been capable of back then. He had been in charge of a couple of Third Division sides before becoming Assistant Manager at Athletic the previous season. Following the previous Manager's sacking after their relegation he had been asked to take on the job himself and he had reluctantly agreed. It might well mean however the end of his dreams of being a top flight manager if he failed to get the team back into the Premiership at the first attempt. The club might be nearly bankrupt following the completion of their new stadium, but it was a club with a big history and expectations were high, very high. No one at the club could have envisaged that only six months after moving to their new state-of-the-art 25,000 capacity stadium they would be out of the Premiership. The ground was part of the Millennium Dome project built at Greenwich to celebrate the arrival of the Year 2000. The Dome and the Athletic Stadium shared the same car park, and the club had thought it would be a great move for them. Maybe they had neglected the playing squad as more and more money got sidetracked for the new ground, but in all honesty they had never looked like being relegated. Athletic had just sort of been sucked into the relegation dogfight right at the end of the season. Even so, they hadn't been in the bottom three at all, except of course, on the very last day. Ironically enough, it was Jim 'Razor' Sharp's last minute goal after coming on as a late substitute for already relegated Forest that had sealed their fate, a draw would have seen them survive the drop. If Jim was worried about what kind of reception he might receive from the Athletic fans he hadn't mentioned it to Blimey.

Jim paid off his taxi and looked around wondering where he should go. Just then he saw the Manager come out of the reception area, no doubt looking for his new star striker who was a bit late, but only a bit.

"Razor," called out the Manager and he walked over and shook Jim warmly by the hand. "I was a bit worried you might not make it. Heard you were in hospital."

"Yeah, I got attacked by an old lady, while I was walking my skinheads."

"What?"

"I got attacked by a dog whilst I was walking my old lady."

"Are you all right?"

"Yeah, I'm fine. Just a little bump on the head. How's things?"

"Pretty crap."

"Same as me then."

"Good then things can only get better. You look like shit by the way. What on earth have you done to yourself?"

"I've let myself go a little bit over the last few years Boss, but I'm here to turn over a new leaf, make a new start. I'm going to be a lean, mean goal-scoring machine by the time the season starts."

"You've got a lot of work to do."

"I'm not afraid of hard work Boss."

"You've had a complete personality change then?"

"I just need to lose a few pounds and I'll be as good as new."

"I hope so. I went against everyone's advice signing you, especially after you scored the goal that got us relegated."

"Just doing my job."

"Well, make sure you do it here too. Come on I'll show you to the changing rooms and introduce you to everyone."

"How many have we got?"

"There are eighteen at the moment, including you."

"Seventeen fit and one unfit then?"

"I'd say more like eighteen unfit, but we're here to change that."

Training began with a half an hour jogging session, round and round a circuit laid out beforehand. The footballers soon split into two distinct groups; the younger, keener, desperate-to-make-a-good-impression players at the front and then, someway farther back, the older seasoned pros who had nothing to prove to anyone, least of all themselves. And finally, lapped by everyone after just five minutes and crawling along on hands and knees after ten, came Razor. In the end, he just sat where he was, panting for breath like a dog, watching the others go past lap after lap. When the half an hour was finally up, he got gingerly to his feet and walked across to rejoin the group.

Then came the thing that Jim hated the most, doggies. They were split into six groups of three and forced to run off in teams, sometimes sprinting, sometimes dribbling a ball or hopping or running backwards. Razor's team predictably lost every time. Finally, after an hour they split into small groups according to their respective positions and Jim found himself with the other two forwards and the three goalkeepers for crossing and then shooting practice. Razor was a shit crosser, it wasn't his thing and never would be, and he was soon told to get in the box to try to put off the keepers as they jumped to catch the crosses that were coming in. First up was the youngest goalie, no doubt recently promoted from the youth team, the one who probably wouldn't play more than a handful of games over the course of the season. A cross came in, hanging invitingly over the penalty spot. This was meat and drink for the great Razor Sharp, and he sprang forward with an agility that surprised everyone. The ball thumped off his forehead and nested tidily in the bottom corner of the net, leaving the young keeper open-mouthed in wonder as to how a man as fat and as out of condition as Jim had managed to get to the ball before him.

There came the sound of applause from across the ground, the Manager had seen what had happened.

"Put in another cross," he called out. A new ball came over and the result was exactly the same. Then a third. Jim was just starting to enjoy himself when the first choice keeper came over and changed places with the youngster.

"Now try," he told Razor. A cross came over, Jim jumped, the goalkeeper jumped, and the ball thumped off Razor's forehead and found the empty net once more, the keeper left sprawling on the ground.

"That's enough," shouted the Manager. "Jim why don't you come out of there and let them get some catching practice? I'd like to have a few words with you."

"Sure Boss," shouted Razor, and he trudged wearily over to the Manager.

"Nice to see you haven't lost your goal-scoring touch Razor."

"It's a gift I've always had," responded the forward modestly.

"We've got a friendly against United in two weeks time, a game to officially open the new stadium, reckon you can be fit for that?"

"United? You bet your life I can be fit."

"They've promised to bring their proper first team squad and use it as a real workout. I want to try out a few things. I'm not sure whether it's best to play four-four-two or four-five-one, so we'll probably give both formations a go in the friendly games we've got. I'll be honest with you Razor, we've known each other a long time, I don't see you as more than a bit-part player in this squad, but I hope that you can use your experience to help out my two young strikers. I see your most likely role as coming on say with fifteen or twenty minutes to go if we're losing, you know, to try to turn things around."

"That's how they used me at Forest," agreed Jim.

"With great effect on the last day of the season."

"I got seven goals from thirteen substitute appearances in a team that was always bottom of the league. Maybe they should have let me start once or twice."

"Obviously I'll need you more if we get injuries or whatever, so, what I'm saying to you is get yourself into match-playing condition. This squad is so small we're going to need every available man and for starters, I'll promise you a good run out against United as long as I see you making an effort to get fit. Okay?"

"Sure Boss. I'd love to stick one in against United. Just for old time's sake."

To end the training session they played a seven-a-side match with rolling substitutes. Jim didn't play much and limited himself to goal hanging when he was on the pitch. He stuck in a couple of half chances that came his way and ended the session feeling quite pleased with himself. Sure the rest of the squad thought he was just a fat old bastard, but at least they knew that the legend of Razor Sharp was for real. Bit-part player indeed, he'd show the Manager he was no bit-part player, and he was going to start by doing a demolition job on the great Manchester United. Razor was actually looking forward to the start of the season, for the first time in ten years.

After a shower he tagged along to the bar with the rest of the squad and the coaching staff. Just a couple of quick pints and then back to the hotel for a rest was Jim's intention, maybe even a swim in the hotel pool. Trouble was, he had always liked a pint after playing, there was nothing more refreshing, and he felt that he deserved it. It was his first drink in thirty-six hours and it seemed to him as if he had been off the booze for a year. The first pint was glorious, the second a delight. By the time he'd had four he felt himself again. He held court there in the leisure club bar, telling his well-honed collection of half-true, half-bullshit anecdotes to anyone who was willing to listen. By six in the afternoon, he ran out of money and realized that everyone from the club had left and there were just a couple of squash players sitting at the bar drinking orange juice.

He stumbled off his stool and headed for the street. He needed to find a bank to get some money.

At nine o'clock the next morning the phone in Razor's room rang. It took him several rings to come round from his coma-like sleep and a lot of fumbling around in the dark to find the bedside table and locate the phone.

"What the fuck?" he asked annoyed at having been woken.

"Your nine o'clock call Mr. Sharp," said the female receptionist crossly.

"Nine o'clock? Already?"

"Yes, Mr. Sharp." The receptionist hung up. Jim was about to lie down and go back to sleep when he remembered what the Manager had told him about playing against United and the need to make an effort in training. Maybe if he scored a hat-trick against them and made United's defence look stupid then they might want to resign him. He laughed out loud at his own joke but it made his head hurt so he quickly stopped. He was hung over as usual. He tried to remember what had happened the previous night and recalled that when he had got some money he had gone to a pub, eaten a large plate of pie and chips and spent the rest of the night drinking whisky with the locals. He took a deep breath to compose himself before getting out of bed so that he wouldn't be sick. A quick shower and a bit of breakfast and he should feel right as rain.

When he arrived at the training ground the other players were already jogging round the day's new circuit. He was late, but then that was what star strikers did. They arrived late for training, ignored what went on in team talks and then went out and won you the match at the weekend. He took his time changing and then walked slowly across the field to see the Manager.

"Morning Boss," he called out cheerfully.

"You're late," replied the Manager.

"Yeah. The hotel forgot my alarm call. Don't worry, I told the bloody receptionist what I thought of her."

"Next time you're late you'll get fined. I run a tight ship here, and you'll get the same treatment as everyone else. I want you to set a good example to the younger players. Now, let's see if you can manage a couple of laps more than yesterday, shall we?"

"We? Are you planning to join me?"

"Me? I've got two totally-fucked knees."

"It would be a good example to the younger players to see their manager taking part."

"You think so?"

"Sure."

"Okay, let's go. Let's see who can do the most laps in what's left of the running session. The loser buys the beers afterwards."

"You're on," said Jim setting off at a slow jog and getting a head start. The Manager soon caught him up. They jogged round together in silence, each trying to convince the other that they weren't feeling any pain. After four and a half laps it was Razor who suddenly collapsed into a heap. He got wearily to his feet and walked on a little bit, but then he had to bend over to be sick. He puked up everything he'd had to eat or drink in the last twenty-four hours, and when there was nothing left he remained bent over dry-retching for a couple of minutes. The club physio walked over with a bucket of water to wash away Jim's pile of puke.

"Bit too much to drink last night Razor?" he laughed.

"No mate, not too much to drink, too much fucking running."

"You'd better get used to it, the Boss likes his players to be fit."

"Much more of this and I'll be dead."

"This is just the start. Next week he's going to introduce stamina work."

"Shit! I've joined the wrong bloody club."

"You could do with losing a few stone you know, not just to make you a better footballer, but for your overall health. And if you want my advice you should give up the booze."

"I've cut back a lot in the last few days," mumbled Jim.

"You seemed to be knocking it back all right yesterday when I left, and by the look of things you didn't stop when you finished here."

"I met some guys in a pub and they insisted on buying me a couple of drinks."

"If you hadn't been in the pub you wouldn't have met them."

"I just popped in to get some change for the taxi."

"Alcoholics lie to justify their drinking Razor, did you know that?"

"Why does everyone keep saying I'm an alcoholic?"

"If everyone's saying it, maybe you ought to start listening."

"I don't need advice from anyone."

"Whatever, it's your life. I just think you owe it to the club to give it a hundred percent for the two years you've got here, that's all."

"I always give it a hundred percent."

"In the bar maybe." The Physio walked away. Jim saw the Manager coming round to lap him. He was ten years Jim's senior and had two fucked-up knees and he was lapping his new star striker. If Razor had problems then his Manager surely had more.

After a week of light training and heavy drinking Jim went on a weekend bender with some Irish guys who were staying at the hotel. They were all United fans and were over the moon to meet a legend such as Razor in the flesh. They took him with them as they toured the pubs and clubs of Central London with their company credit cards. These guys knew how to drink, but Razor matched them Guinness for Guinness, whisky for whisky.

Stamina training began on Monday morning. Jim arrived half an hour late looking like death and promptly got a bollocking from the Manager and his first fine. He tried to take part in the bleep test, but got bleeped out in a couple of minutes. He'd never been good at bleep tests. What was the fucking point of bleep tests for Christ's sake? Did bleep tests make you a better footballer? Would a bleep test help Jim to be more aware in the opposition's penalty area? Would it make him deadlier in front of goal? Of course it wouldn't. Who was the sad sicko who dreamed up the bleep test? Fucking sadist bastard. Jim sat by the side of the pitch and watched his teammates slowly drop out of the bleep test one after another. Each one falling knackered onto the grass when they couldn't take anymore. They had to be crazy the lot of them.

While they were sitting quietly in a group recovering from their ordeal, a black Porsche, shiny and new, pulled into the car park. The driver killed the powerful engine and then a young black guy emerged from behind the tinted windows. The newcomer raised his sunglasses onto the top of his head and looked across the field to where the Manager was. He raised an arm in salute and the Manager hurried over to greet him.

"Who the fuck is that?" Jim asked the Physio.

"That's our new signing, haven't you heard? We just got the first part of our parachute payment from the FA. That's what the Manager decided to spend it on."

"Who is he?"

"Leonard Malloy. Top scorer in the Second Division last season."

"A striker?"

"'Fraid so Jim," laughed the Physio, "that makes you fourth choice I should think."

"Fourth choice? Fuck off. He's only a kid. How old is he? Twelve?"

"Nineteen, nearly twenty."

"When I was nineteen I was Manchester United's top scorer for the season I got twenty goals."

"That was then and this is now," said the Physio with a shrug.

Jim looked across the field and saw the Manager fawning over his new signing, it was enough to make you want to puke, if you hadn't done so already of course.

The Manager eventually emerged from the sports centre with an arm around his new young signing, almost like they were father and son. The Manager introduced Leonard to the rest of the squad.

"Hi everyone, sorry I'm a bit late. It's good to be here."

"You gonna fine him for being late?" asked Jim.

"Shut up Razor," snapped the Manager quickly.

"What Boss? So it's one rule for me and a different one for everyone else?"

"You've been late six days running. It's not as if you haven't had enough time to get your act in gear."

Razor knew when to shut up and did so. The Manager decided they should go on a run, which basically meant lapping the playing fields they were using for pre-season training. The squad reluctantly got up and everyone headed off after the Assistant Manager who was a forty year old ex-Chelsea player turned fitness freak. From his place at the back of the pack, Jim could make out the club's new signing loping along on the leader's shoulder.

"Bastard missed the bleep test," muttered Razor to no one in particular.

"So did you brother," someone called back over their shoulder.

123

Jim trudged on wearily, right around the edge of the huge playing fields where they trained, completely on his own, either jogging very slowly or walking quickly it was hard to say, but he stuck to his guns and managed to do the whole circuit. When he got back to the start he found the rest already doing doggies, his place taken by Leonard Malloy. Razor wondered if it was worth ringing Blimey Brown to see if he had thought to put a 'no new strikers' clause in his contract, but no doubt not even Blimey was that good.

After the doggies, the whole squad sat in the shade of a huge tree and listened as the Manager talked about the different formations he planned to try out in the three friendly games the club had arranged before the start of the season proper, the first one being the visit of the great Manchester United. Maybe if this Leonard kid played well, United would want to sign him and get him out of Jim's hair. Jim could more or less handle starting the season as third striker, sitting on the bench in the sunshine, coming on for little twenty minute cameos, grabbing a few late goals and a few headlines and keeping the fans on his side until he got his chance to get into the starting line up. But fourth striker, what the hell was that? He'd be cleaning boots with the youth team and carrying Leonard's massive kitbag from his Porsche to the dressing rooms or something. No, fourth striker was not a role for the legendary Razor Sharp.

At the end of the session, they played seven-a-side as usual, and Jim found himself impatiently waiting on the touchline as Leonard showed off his skills by banging in four or five quick goals. They weren't great goals, he obviously wasn't a natural finisher like Jim had always been, but what he did have was pace. In the lower divisions pace would have got him through on goal several times in a game, so as long as he could get a shot in on target, he would no doubt end up with a few goals. The keepers weren't so good down in the lower leagues either. Jim wondered if Leonard had enough pace to be able to get away from higher quality defenders.

The Manager called his new striker off and Jim got his chance at last, but his teammates had got lazy with the luxury of Leonard's pace and insisted on kicking the ball through into space for Jim to run onto. That wasn't Razor's game and he wasn't about to go chasing lost causes, especially in a kick about match. Jim needed the ball to feet and no further out than the edge of the penalty area if he was going to get the chance of a shot at goal. The training session finished and the players headed wearily for the showers.

Exhausted under a hot stream of water, Razor found himself wondering which would be the best injury to fake to get out of this awful stamina training, but of course there was still a chance that he might get a few precious minutes against United if he stuck it out. If he scored against them he would instantly get the Athletic fans on his side, friendly game or not. He'd just have to grit his teeth and get through the remaining days of stamina.

When he was changed, Razor made his way to the bar. Just a quick beer and then back to the hotel for a sauna he thought. Maybe later he'd go somewhere for a nice massage, not the kind of massage the club physio would give you for a thigh strain, but a real massage from some big busty blonde with extras extra. That's what he needed to build up his stamina, not bleep tests and endless laps of a field for fuck's sake.

"Can I join you?" came a voice from beside him. Jim looked up to see the club's new signing.

"Sure. Beer?"

"No, thanks, an orange squash for me, I don't drink."

"An orange squash for my new girlfriend," Razor called out to the barman.

"Tell me about United Razor, I want to know what it's like to play for United."

"It's okay," said Jim.

"Only okay?"

"What do you want me to say? United's the greatest club in the world. I'd give my right testicle to be your age again and be back at United, the left one too come to think of it, they're fuck all use to me now anyway."

"That good huh?"

"Better."

"I wanna play for United. If I can score the goals to get Athletic back in the Premiership then I'll have a chance to impress United next season."

"You really think this pathetic shower of shit can get back into the Premiership?"

"Yeah man, this shower of shit and me and the great Razor Sharp, why not?"

"Don't think I'll be playing too much," said Jim.

"The Manager told me you were critical to his plans. He reckons that you and I will make a deadly partnership, my pace and your finishing."

"Told me he had me down as a bit-part player."

"He's playing mind games with you. He wants to keep you keen in training. You've seen the other two forwards out there today, they're nothing special. They're the bit-part players, not you and I. If they were any good, the team wouldn't have gotten relegated."

"I relegated them," stated Jim. Leonard burst out laughing.

"I know, funny isn't it? That's probably why they didn't want to give you a decent pass out there today, you got them all a twenty-five percent wage cut!"

FOUR

Jim stuck with stamina training as best he could. Leonard was staying in the same hotel, so he gave Razor a lift to training every day and managed to drive fast enough to get them there on time, despite Jim's best efforts to make them late. Being late for training was what star strikers did, it was expected of them, but Leonard was too damn keen by half.

With Leonard to prize him away from the leisure club bar after a couple of beers, Razor found himself with long afternoons ahead of him, and when Leonard went down to the hotel gymnasium Jim went with him and lazily pumped a few weights or sat idly on an exercise bike watching his younger team mate work out. Sometimes, he would fall into the heated pool and lie in the shallow end, just occasionally swimming an unhurried length or two. What did him good more than anything was being away from smoky pubs and hours of drinking. In the evenings, Leonard would head off for central London in search of excitement and Jim would hold court in the hotel bar, but more often than not he would only have the barman for company, and after a few beers he would head up to his own room and watch TV, drinking whisky from the minibar and chain smoking.

Early Friday afternoon, as he lay resting on his bed after a light training session, the phone rang.

"You have a call Mr. Sharp, it's Angie," said the receptionist.

"Hi Jim," came Angie's voice.

"How are you?"

"Not so bad, all things considered. Listen, I thought I'd bring Mikey down for the weekend, he said he'd like to see you play against United, and you and I need to talk."

"Talk about what?"

"'Bout what's going to happen with Mikey. I think it's best if he goes to a boarding school in London, that way he'll only have to be with you during the holidays. Can you book us into your hotel 'til Monday?"

"No problem, I'll do it right away."

"Okay, we'll get the train down in a couple of hours or so. I'll ring you when I know what time the train gets in."

"Yeah, we can get something to eat."
"You won't get pissed will you?"
"No, I won't, you won't recognize me. I'm a new man."
"I'll believe that when I see it."
"You'll see."

Jim hung up the phone and caught sight of himself in the mirror. His beard was wild, his hair unruly, his eyebrows like crazed caterpillars. He returned to the phone and made a reservation for Angie and Mikey and then asked to be put through to Leonard's room.

"It's Razor."
"Yeah? You ready for the gym?"
"Nah, fuck the gym, listen, where d'you get your hair cut?"
"Haircut? You want a haircut?"
"Yeah. A haircut, a shave, the works."
"God Razor, you sure?"
"Sure."
"When was the last time you had a haircut man?"
"When I was in prison, I guess."
"You were in prison?"
"Yeah. Why? Did you think I was some sort of goody goody or something?"
"No, course not, no one would think that of you."
"Right. So, do you know a good barber's or not?"
"You mean a hairdresser's?"
"Whatever, I leave it in your hands. Set up an appointment as soon as you can and call me back."

The young people in the hairdressing salon almost dropped dead when Jim walked in.

"Who did this to you darling?" asked a young man who looked like a doctor in a white lab coat.
"He just call me darling?" Jim asked Leonard.
"Don't worry he didn't mean anything."
"He calls me darling again, I'll break his face."
"What did sir have in mind?" asked the hairdresser.
"Make him look human again, if you can," suggested Leonard.

"Very short," decided Jim, "and get rid of the beard and the eyebrows."
"Would you like us to dye it for you darl..., sir?"
"Dye what?"
"Your hair sir. We can get rid of the grey for you."
"Do whatever you want, just make me look respectable."
"Would sir like a coffee while we discuss styles?"
"Sure," said Jim, "I'm here for the full treatment."

It took a long time, and luckily Leonard had thought to book a double appointment, but in the end Razor really did look like a new man.
"Good god, look at you!" exclaimed Leonard looking up from a car magazine he had been reading.
"Do I look respectable?"
"Like a fucking accountant or maybe a bank clerk or something."
"You don't think maybe it's a bit over the top?"
"Well, it's different from the old you, for sure, I think it's one hell of an improvement though."
"Will Angie like it?"
"She like you ten years ago?"
"I guess so."
"Then she'll like you now man. These people have just made you look like a twenty year old."
"Thanks Leonard."
"No sweat man, all you need now is some new clothes."
"Clothes? What's wrong with my clothes?"
"What's right with 'em?"
"Shit. They that bad?"
"Worse. You're lucky you're a footballer and you only appear on tele in football kit."
"I used to get invited on chat shows, you know?"
"Really?"
"Yeah. I was on Wogan twice."
"What's Wogan?"
"Oh nothing. Don't worry. We got time to look for some new trousers or something?"

129

"Reckon so, if we're quick. I'll drop you at the station, so don't worry 'bout that."

They left the hairdresser's and walked down the street a bit to a clothes shop. It was part of a national chain, not a boutique or anything exclusive, but Leonard thought that Razor just needed something normal-looking rather than anything too flash. After all, he was going to meet his ex-wife and son, not going on a hot date.

Jim ended up with a pair of dark grey trousers and a white shirt and some new black leather shoes. He came out of the dressing room in his new gear, the labels in his hands, which he took to the till.

"Shall I put your old clothes in a bag?" offered the shop assistant, not too used to customers wearing their new clothes out of the shop.

"Nah, throw it all away," Leonard told him.

"Very good sir," came the reply.

They sped through the streets of London to the station and Jim arrived just in time to find the right platform as the train was pulling in. He stood by the exit barrier and looked for Angie. It wasn't long before he saw her, pulling along a small case in one hand, holding Mikey's hand with the other. Jim was about to wave to them and call out, but suddenly he stopped himself. He stood still where he was and watched them as they neared the exit. Angie was scanning the crowd beyond the barrier, looking for her ex-husband, and she didn't give Jim a second glance, why should she? She was looking for a bearded gorilla of a man who always looked as if he had been in a fight with a haystack and been soundly beaten. Angie and Mikey passed through the exit and both stood looking a little lost as they desperately searched for Jim.

Eventually, Angie caught sight of the man who was looking at her, smiling from ear to ear, an idiotic look on his face.

"Hi Angie," he said at last, unable to prevent himself any longer. Angie's jaw dropped open, Mikey's did too.

"No. It can't be."

"It is."

"No. Jim? Surely not!"

"Yep, it's me. What d'you think?"

"Oh my god! What have you done to yourself?"

"Don't you like it?"

130

"Course I like it. It's just that you look completely different that's all."
"What do you think Mikey?" he asked his son.
"You look like new, Jim," replied the boy.
"See, I told you I was a new man Angie."
"Yeah, but I never thought you meant it."
"And I'm not drunk."

Angie reached up on tiptoes and kissed Jim's new face, and then she slipped her arm into his and let him lead her out of the station. Mikey trailed behind dragging the case.

Before the match the following afternoon, Jim took Mikey into the Manchester United dressing room to meet some of the world's most famous players.

"That's never you Razor, is it?" asked the United Manager who was the same one who had told Jim that he no longer had a future with the Red Devils. Razor just smiled, he'd already had the who the hell are you? Routine from his teammates in the other dressing room. Indeed, every time he caught sight of his reflection in a mirror he couldn't believe it himself.

"Razor, good to see you," called out the United captain who had been a mere youngster when Jim had last played in their team. Jim shook his hand and introduced him to his little son. Mikey, overawed in the presence of such a superstar, just offered his little autograph book and a pen. The United captain took it and whipped off a quick scribble as professional footballers were used to doing, and then passed the book onto the United and England centre forward. He was a young man with the world at his feet, barely out of his teens and with a talent that took people's breath away. He reminded Jim of himself ten years before. What the hell had gone wrong? Razor knew the answer, booze. He'd always liked a drink and staying out late, and it hadn't been a problem until he got injured. With the lack of exercise forced upon him by the specialists as they waited for his knee to heal after all the operations, the depression that engulfed him as he came to terms with not playing, and hours with nothing much to do, so he began to drink more and more until it took over his life.

Mikey's autograph book did the rounds and eventually came back to him, and then Jim took him up to the main stand to find his mother. Looking down onto the bright green of the pitch from the height of the stand, Jim realized what a fantastic stadium London Athletic had got. As close to the river as Fulham's Craven Cottage, right next to the almost-completed Millennium Dome, it had to be one of the best in England. There was no doubt that the club should be in the Premiership, and Jim resolved there and then to do his part in making it happen.

When he got back to the Athletic changing room, he found his teammates all ready to go out. Quickly he put on his kit and then zipped up a tracksuit top as both he and Leonard would be starting on the subs bench. It was no surprise really, they were the new faces and had to earn their way into the starting line up. The other two strikers had both been with the club for several seasons and were two of the few recognized players who hadn't done a runner the moment the club had been relegated.

The noise was fantastic as the teams took to the pitch. Every United fan in London had tried to get a ticket and the game was a sell-out. Not bad for a pre-season friendly in the middle of the cricket season, but such was the draw of the great Manchester United.

The match kicked off and United predictably took control, majestic and calm like a cat toying with a mouse it doesn't yet want to kill. The crowd, more United than Athletic, oohed and aahed at every completed pass, at every little flick or feint and applauded rapturously every attempt on goal.

"Thank god we won't be playing against this lot every week," whispered Leonard to Razor as they sat in the dugout.

"Yeah, our forwards haven't had a pass, have they?" replied Jim.

"No. I'm glad I'm on the bench."

"Me too," lied Razor.

By half time Athletic were three goals down and hadn't registered a single shot on target of their own. In the changing room during in the break the Manager tried to motivate his players to get forward more, but as they rightly pointed out, if they didn't have the ball it was difficult to pass it forward. Jim thought he might get on at half time, but it wasn't to be. The Manager changed two midfielders in the hope that some fresh legs in that department might get them a bit more possession. It didn't work. Even though United had substituted four of their best players, including their England centre forward, they still scored two more goals in the first fifteen minutes of the second period.

"Razor and Leonard start warming up," the Manager told them as the fifth goal went in. Five minutes later, he told Leonard to strip off and get ready for action. The fans applauded generously as Leonard took to the pitch, he was the club's only money signing of the summer and all hope of promotion was pinned on him. Could he reproduce the goal scoring form he had shown in the lower divisions?

The minutes ticked by. United scored a sixth goal. The Manager pulled off a midfielder and the other forward who had started the game and put on two defenders. Six was bad enough, but he didn't want it to be ten. Friendly or no friendly, conceding so many goals was not going to be good for anyone's morale.

Jim got fed up with standing on the touchline supposedly warming up and went back to the dugout. He shot the Manager his 'I'm starting to get seriously pissed off' look, but the Manager didn't seem to notice.

"Want a run Razor?" the Manager finally asked him with about twelve minutes left.

"That's what I fucking came for," snapped Jim.

"Calm down, just get yourself ready." Razor stood up and took off his tracksuit top.

"Ready Boss."

The Manager led him to the side of the pitch.

"I want you to slot into the middle of midfield. Sit just in front of the back four and don't let anyone get past you. We're getting pissed on, it's time to shut up shop."

"I'm not a tackler Boss," said Jim.

"Do your best." The ball went out of play and the substitution was made. Jim's introduction was met with almost complete silence on the part of the Athletic fans, but by a rousing chorus of who ate all the pies from the massed United ranks. Razor was not a happy man. Someone was going to pay.

He told the other players where the Manager wanted him to be and moodily went and slotted in at the back of the midfield. He wasn't planning on moving very far, he was just going to tackle anyone who came near him. He didn't have to wait very long for his first opportunity, since United soon put together a typically fluent passing move and began coming forward through the centre. One of the United youngsters, on for the last half an hour, ran at Jim and made the mistake of pushing the ball through Razor's legs and trying to run round him. That pissed Jim off even more, and he stepped across his opponent's path, dug his elbow deep into the youngster's ribs and sent his sprawling to the ground. Suddenly, all hell broke loose, four or five United players rounded on Razor, pushing and shoving him. The Referee came over to try to intervene. Someone put a hand in Jim's face and he lashed out a fist in blind self-defence. There was a huge roar from the crowd and when the hand was removed from his face Jim saw that he had accidently laid out the Ref. The United players backed away leaving Razor guiltily standing over the prostrate match official. Both trainers hurried onto the field, as did the two assistants.

"You're really for it Razor," hissed the Athletic Physio as he knelt down to attend to the Ref.

"What the fuck have you done?" Leonard wanted to know.

"Just piss off," snarled Jim who was still wound up.

Eventually, with the aid of some smelling salts, the Ref came round and sat up. He tried to remember what was going on, but in the end he had to allow himself to be helped off the pitch by the two physios. The crowd gave him a rousing send off with a tuneful chorus of the referee's a wanker as he disappeared down the tunnel. The fourth official finally made his way out onto the pitch to see through the remaining ten minutes of the game. He headed straight for Razor and waved a red card in his face.

"Hey, fucking hell, it was an accident," complained Jim.

"Get off the pitch now, before you make things worse for yourself," the new referee instructed him.

"Come on Razor, get out of here man," Leonard advised him.

"You can fuck off," shouted Razor in his face. Leonard backed away.

"Whatever you say, but your kid's watching remember."

"What do I care who's watching?"

"Are you leaving? Or do I have to put in my report that you refused to go?" the fourth official wanted to know.

"It was an accident," mumbled Jim, but even he was beginning to realise that he wasn't going to play any further part in the game. His debut had lasted maybe forty-five seconds, and he hadn't even touched the ball. The Razor Sharp legend had well and truly hit rock bottom.

"I'll 'ave you next time we play," Razor shouted at one of the United players who he thought might have been responsible.

"I don't think you'll ever play in the Premiership again you fat bastard," the player retorted. The remark just bounced off Jim's broad back as he walked slowly off the field. He was surprised to hear the crowd applauding him as he neared the touchline and as he entered the tunnel they cheered him. After all, it wasn't every day that someone decked a referee.

Razor had just sat down in the changing room when the Manager stormed in.

"You stupid bloody bastard!" spat the Manager who was bright red in the face and looked as if he were about to explode. "They'll probably ban you for life, you realize that, don't you?"

"It was an accident Boss."

"Accident my arse. As far as I'm concerned you're finished at this club. I'll be talking to the directors in the morning about getting you fired. How does that sound to you?"

"I didn't mean to do it. Someone put their hand in my face and I just lashed out. It was self defence. I didn't even know the Ref was there."

"Save the bullshit for the FA. They're gonna throw the book at you. You're finished. You should do the honourable thing and quit. Get the hell out of here before the match finishes and get out of my sight." The Manager left. Razor took off his boots, pulled on a tracksuit and some trainers and went to find Angie and Mikey. He found them in the club lounge.

"Oh my god. I can't believe you punched the referee. What were you thinking?"

"Maybe I'm gonna quit," said Jim.

"Let's get back to the hotel before you do anything else stupid today. You need to talk to Bill about this. He'll know what to do."

"Not even Blimey Brown can save me this time."

FIVE

If the match hadn't been against United, no doubt there wouldn't have been such a fuss surrounding Jim Sharp in the days afterwards, but wherever the great Manchester United went, the press went too. There was also television evidence since the London ITV company had bought the rights to show limited highlights of the game on their nightly news and sports programme. So, Razor laying out a referee became London's headline story that very same night and grabbed the back pages of the following morning's papers.

Razor holed up in his room with Angie and Mikey whilst the press camped downstairs in the hotel bar. Everyone was waiting for Bill Brown to arrive.

At last, mid-morning, the phone rang in Jim's room. It was reception, who had been told not to disturb him for anyone except his agent, Blimey was on his way up. Jim opened the door and watched his friend stride manfully down the corridor. He looked determined and purposeful and that was just what Razor had always liked about him, but more than anything he had the knack of making bad things go away, like some miracle-working father of an extremely naughty child.

"Blimey Razor, you've fucking gone and done it this time," shouted the agent as soon as he reckoned he was within ear shot. Jim didn't reply. It was best to let the man have a bit of a rant and rave in order to clear his head. Anyway, Jim deserved all he was going to get.

It was Angie who came to the footballer's rescue by grabbing Blimey by the arm as he entered the room and steering him towards the couch.

"Sit down," she told him, "I'll make us all a cup of coffee and we'll talk this through, but I don't want any shouting and I don't want any swearing. Is that understood?" she said indicating her son with an outstretched arm. Mikey was watching cartoons on the TV with the volume turned down low.

Blimey sat down. Jim sank into an armchair just out of punching range and decided to keep very quiet. His agent sat glaring across at him, steam almost coming out of his ears as he tried desperately to control his temper.

"It was supposed to be my day off," he hissed. "My first day off in five years. I wasn't going to do anything special, just sort of do nothing, you know?"

"Sorry mate," said Jim.

"Sorry? I should think you're fucking sorry."

"Blimey!" snapped Angie.

"Sorry," said Blimey. "Maybe Razor and I should talk in private."

"No, any decisions about Jim's future will be made with my approval."

"She's right," agreed Razor who had no desire to be left alone at the mercy of Blimey's temper.

"Since when do you care about his future? You two aren't back together or something are you?"

"Good god no," said Angie, "definitely not. Listen Bill, I guess it's time you knew what's happening. It'll make things easier to understand."

"What's up?"

"I'm dying. I've got cancer and I've only got a few months to live."

"Oh Jesus Angie, no."

"Yes, I've had all the tests and tried all the treatments and there's nothing that can be done. That's why I'm here, to sort things out with Jim."

"I'm so sorry," whispered Blimey and he got to his feet and went over to Angie and took her into his arms. "What can I say?"

"Just say you'll continue to look after Jim's affairs, for the sake of my son."

"Blimey! I must confess that I came here to tell Razor that I wasn't going to be his agent anymore."

"I thought you might, but he needs you now, our son needs you. We've known each other for a long time, there's no one else I trust like you."

"Okay, I'll face the flack, but it's the last time. I won't keep bailing him out of trouble , not anymore. If he doesn't make an effort, a really big effort, then he'll be on his own."

"I'll try," offered Razor.

"So, what are our options?" asked Angie.

"Options?"

"Yeah. What can we do?"

"I'd say that our options are pretty limited," Blimey informed her.

"There must be something you can suggest. You've been in this game a long time."

"I've never had a client who punched a referee before. In fact, Jim's the only client I've ever had who's punched anyone, and he went to jail the last time."

"I was provoked," put in Razor and instantly wished he'd kept his mouth shut.

"Best if you keep quiet and let us think," Angie told him. Jim sat back in his chair and closed his eyes. Maybe, if he kept them closed for long enough then all his troubles would just disappear.

"What if we tell the press that I've got terminal cancer and that Jim's been under a lot of stress lately? That might get them on our side."

"It's not the press we have to worry about this time," responded Blimey. "I spoke to the club this morning, there's an emergency director's meeting at two o'clock to decide if they should sack Jim or not."

"Can they sack him?"

"They could, but I wouldn't make it easy for them. I'd hold out for every penny of his contract and they probably already know that."

"If that's our worst case scenario then it's not as bad as I thought," decided Angie, "at least he'll get two years wages out of it."

"Only if they sack him. They'll more than likely offer him a deal, but they can't afford two years salary. They've just spent several million on Leonard Malloy."

"So, they won't sack him?"

"No, I don't think so. Most likely they'll wait for the FA to ban him for life, and then they can terminate his contract without paying a penny."

"They can do that?"

"Jim signed a contract to play football, if he can't play because he's banned then he's in breach of contract. Simple as that."

"And then they won't pay him a penny?"

"No. Nothing."

"Christ. This is all I need." Angie suddenly broke down and burst into tears. Mikey, seeing her crying, rushed to her and started crying too, his arms wrapped around her.

"Can I say something?" asked Razor.

139

"Is it something constructive?" sobbed his ex-wife wiping away some tears with the back of her hand.

"I'm innocent. I didn't mean to punch the referee, I didn't know he was there. I couldn't even see, someone had their hand in my face."

"But you still threw a punch," said Blimey.

"Yes I did, and that was stupid, but I didn't mean to punch the referee."

"Will anyone believe him Bill?" asked Angie.

"I really doubt it," decided the agent.

"There are TV pictures for Christ's sake. All we do is show the video and convince the FA that the referee wasn't the person I was trying to punch."

"The pictures were from a long way away weren't they?" asked Angie.

"Yeah, but they can be blown up, can't they?" said Jim.

"Yes, I expect they can," agreed Blimey.

"That's it then," declared Angie. "We hit the FA with a double attack, my cancer and the TV footage, it might work."

"Maybe," said Blimey thoughtfully. "He's still going to get the book thrown at him for gross violent misconduct, and it's not as if he doesn't have previous."

"What's the worst they can do to him?" Angie wanted to know.

"A ban, obviously."

"Obviously. How long?"

"I don't know. If Jim pleads guilty to violent misconduct, that might help a bit. There'll be a fine too, of course."

"Of course."

"It was only a friendly," moaned Jim.

"I don't think that will help too much," Blimey informed him.

"What about the club?" asked Angie.

"I expect they'll offer Razor a deal, like I was saying, try to get him to quit."

"Which he won't do."

"In which case, I expect they'll suspend him until the hearing."

"When will the hearing be?"

"It's a case that's grabbed the headlines, I expect the FA will want to get it sorted out in the coming week."

"Good," said Jim. "The sooner it's sorted out, the sooner I can be playing again."

"Prepare yourself for the worst Razor. To be honest I don't think you'll ever play football again. What a way to end a career," said Blimey.

"It's kind of fitting if you ask me," put in Angie.

"I'll beat this thing," decided Jim. "I'll beat this and play again, and I'll be a great player again, you'll see."

Angie and Bill exchanged doubtful glances, but left it at that.

"Let's go ask to speak to the directors," decided Blimey, "rather than wait to be called. Let them see we're being positive. Jim, ring reception and order a taxi, let's get going. I like the haircut by the way, nice idea Angie."

"Wasn't my idea, but he looks ten years younger, don't you think?"

"Yeah, he only looks fifty-five now."

Jim and Blimey sat and waited outside the board room at the club's beautiful new ground by the Millennium Dome. Not all the directors had arrived yet, but those that had, had made it more than clear to Razor that they were not happy at having to hold an emergency meeting on his account. The manager arrived.

"Come to quit?" he asked Jim. "You should do the honourable thing and save everyone a lot of time."

"My client's not a quitter," Bill Brown informed him.

"Your client's a fucking idiot," retorted the manager, and he entered the boardroom.

"I get the feeling that he's not on my side," mumbled Jim.

"No one's on your side, not even me," Blimey told him.

Finally, when everyone had turned up, a stormy meeting began. The two men sitting outside could clearly hear the sound of raised voices and waves of arguments surging back and forth, but they couldn't make out what exactly was being said. Jim would have given anything that he owned at that moment for a bottle of whisky, but even he knew that now was not the moment to get drunk. After about forty-five minutes things went quiet and then the door opened. Jim and Blimey went in. They were shown seats at the end of the long table. Jim sat down but Blimey remained standing.

"We've come to the conclusion that the best thing for all concerned is for you to resign Jim," the Chairman stated matter-of-factly. "If you do that, then attention will be removed from the club, and in return we're prepared to offer you a fair deal. A very fair deal."

"How much?" asked Blimey.

"Well, all things considered, we think that three month's wages would be more than generous."

"Three months?"

"Yes, Mr. Brown, it's possible that the FA will ban your client for life, in which case his contract becomes null and void. At best, they might ban him for say five years. He's not a young man, it doesn't look like he'll ever play football again."

Jim suddenly realized that he liked football. Or at least he couldn't think of anything else he could do for the rest of his life. Most footballers of his age had already begun to make retirement plans. Some decided to open sports shops or to go into marketing or public relations. Some wanted to become agents, some media pundits, and the more foolish might start taking coaching exams to prepare themselves for management, but what the fuck could Jim Sharp do after football? Certainly none of the obvious things. His image was so tarnished that no company, club, newspaper or TV channel would ever want anything to do with him. If he opened a pub he'd just drink away the profits and never leave the building. He wasn't exactly sure about his financial situation, but he was certain that there wasn't enough in the bank for him to retire on. Sure, in his glory days he'd been amongst the highest-paid professionals in the country, but his love of fast cars and even faster women hadn't left much for a rainy day, and today it was positively pissing down. If he were negotiating for himself, then he would take the three months being offered, buy a lorry-load of whisky, lock himself in some cheap hotel room and drink himself to death. Fortunately, Bill Brown, the best agent in London, was doing the deals.

"My client's not here to quit Mr. Chairman," said Blimey puffing himself up to his full height. "His punching the referee was an accident and we intend to prove that to the Football Association."

"How will you do that?"

"We'll use the TV pictures to clear his name. At the time of the incident, Jim had a hand in his face and reacted in self defence. It was unfortunate that the referee happened to be on the receiving end, but he wasn't the intended target."

"And you really think the FA will swallow that?"

"It's the truth," Blimey told the Board.

"Six months," offered the Chairman. "That's our final deal. He hasn't even played in a proper match for us for Christ's sake."

"Thank you, but no. My client signed for this club to play football, to score goals. That's what he does. He scored ninety-two goals for Manchester United in 183 games. Last season he scored seven goals in just thirteen substitute appearances for a side that got relegated."

"One of those goals got us relegated," said the Chairman.

"Then you know firsthand what he's still capable of."

"The FA won't be soft on him Mr. Brown, the press are baying for his blood."

"We've got something to get the press off his back."

"Really? I'd like to hear about that."

"You will, we're calling a press conference this afternoon."

"So, Jim isn't going to quit then?" asked the Chairman sounding extremely disappointed.

"No sir, my client's not a quitter."

"He'll never play in my side again," snorted the Manager jumping to his feet.

"Then you've got yourself a very expensive boot cleaner for the next two years."

"We'll transfer list him."

"Who'll have him?" asked Blimey with a little laugh.

The Manager sat down. He knew he was beaten, although he was still convinced that the FA would get rid of Jim Sharp for him.

"The Club cannot be seen to support someone who punched a referee," put in the Chairman, "you understand that Mr. Brown, we're a family club."

"Of course Mr. Chairman. That's why you have no alternative than to suspend my client until after the hearing."

"You really think he'll beat this?"

143

"If I didn't I'd take the six months on offer."

"That's it then. We might as well do a joint press conference this afternoon."

"It's good to present a united front on this," said Blimey, instantly wishing he hadn't used the word 'united.'

SIX

Outside F.A. Headquarters, all was hustle and bustle. With the new season just days away, football was very much at the forefront of the nation's mind. The press were gearing up for another nine months of creating and destroying heroes, of sniffing out scandals and of hounding the current beleaguered England Manager. No one wanted anyone to succeed and therefore anyone who was successful was viewed with suspicion and dislike, and was not permitted a moment's respite until they made a mistake and everything went to pot.

The press had gathered en masse for the final nail in the coffin of the former Manchester United superstar, Jim 'Razor' Sharp. There was nothing they liked better than when the great heroes crashed and burned, and Razor's fall had been as big as any that had gone before him. Problems with alcohol, rumours of drug-taking, gambling, players who cheated on their wives, footballers who were homosexuals, it all paled into insignificance against what Razor had done. No one could ever remember a professional player in England having punched a referee before. This was big. If the FA handed down a lifetime ban then there were hundreds of columns of print to be written charting the decline and fall of Old Trafford's former blue-eyed boy.

Blimey bundled Razor into the building by a rear entrance and advised him not to say anything at all if he could possibly help it. The agent had with him a copy of the video tape of the incident and another of a boxing match where a fighter had also accidently punched the referee. He wasn't sure that it would help, after all, punches were expected to be thrown in boxing, but it was worth a try.

The referee from the game was there along with his two assistants and the fourth official who had actually been the one to send Razor off. There was a three man FA panel and a secretary to take down the details of what went on. The charge of assaulting a referee was read out and Jim was asked whether or not he wanted to contest the charge against him.

"My client wishes to acknowledge violent misconduct on a football pitch, for which he will accept the appropriate punishment. But he didn't mean to punch the referee."

"And you think you can prove that?" asked one of the panel raising a bushy grey eyebrow.

"Let's take a look at a couple of video tapes, shall we?"

A TV and video were waiting at the side of the room and Blimey walked across and inserted the first of his tapes. To everyone's surprise, it wasn't a football match at all. They watched as a boxer, his face lowered towards the canvas, swung a wild dying punch just as the referee stepped in to save him from further punishment. The punch caught the referee full in the face and felled him to the ground.

"It's happened before you see," said Blimey.

"But Mr. Brown, you can't confuse boxing with football, your client had no right to swing a punch on a football field."

"Of course not, and he sincerely regrets his actions."

Everyone looked at Jim and he nodded in agreement, trying to look as sincere as possible. To be honest he was feeling very scared, scared that they would never allow him to be involved in football again, scared that he would be dumped on life's scrap heap.

"And your other video Mr. Brown?"

"This is the video of the actual incident," continued Blimey, replacing the boxing tape with the football one. "Imagine if you will a man who is desperate to make an impression at his new club. A man playing against former team mates, and a man who the previous day had learnt that his ex-wife, the mother of his eight year old boy is dying of cancer. I hope, gentlemen, to some degree you can appreciate my client's frame of mind at the time of this unfortunate incident."

"There can be no excuse for punching a referee," said someone.

The video began. The young United player ran towards Jim, slipped the ball through his legs and was taken down. A crowd instantly formed around Razor, pushing and shoving him. Blimey paused the video and pointed out the hand covering Jim's face. The next second, as the tape continued, the referee came into the picture and Razor swung his blind punch. Blimey rewound the tape and let the incident play again and again, like the bullet that took off Kennedy's head, leaving no one in any doubt that the referee had not been the intended target.

"Have you anything further to add?" Blimey was asked.

"No. Gentlemen I think you will agree that the pictures speak for themselves."

"Then would you and your client please wait outside whilst we consider a decision."

Jim sat, nervously biting his nails, whilst Blimey returned some calls on his mobile which he had had switched off during the hearing. His page three stunner had a problem. She had just made it big and now she was pregnant. Blimey was trying to convince her that there were still newspapers and magazines that would pay her to pose naked being pregnant, but she was inconsolable. She didn't even know who the father was.

At last they were called back in. Jim took a big deep breath as he sat down. In his head he could hear the clang, clang, clang of a single bell chiming a death knell.

"We accept Mr. Brown, that it wasn't your client's intention to punch the referee, but we do find him guilty of extreme violent misconduct. Owing to his previous disciplinary problems, we feel we have no choice but to ban him from playing for ten weeks."

"From the date of the incident?" asked Blimey immediately.

"From the date of the incident," confirmed the official.

"Ten weeks," mumbled Jim.

"Did you wish to say something Mr. Sharp?" he was asked.

"My client just wants to say thank you for hearing his case so promptly, and to apologise to the referee and to the F.A. for any embarrassment he may have caused. Thank you all."

Blimey hauled Jim to his feet and dragged him out of the room before the result could be changed. They waited while the F.A.'s Press Secretary briefed the media with the result, and then Blimey led Razor before the cameras.

It was Blimey who expressed Jim's regret for his actions, his deep sorrow at having dragged the good name of his new club through the mud and his humble acceptance of the FA's punishment. It was Blimey who reassured the Athletic fans that as soon as his ban was over, Jim would be scoring the goals to take them back to the Premier League where they belonged. Jim just sat and said nothing. Ten weeks just kept going through his mind. Ten long, agonising, weeks. It felt as if he had been handed a life sentence.

They went by taxi back to the club and were shown up to the boardroom where the Chairman and the Manager were waiting for them. They had obviously seen the result of the hearing on Sky News which was playing quietly on a TV in the corner.

"Congratulations Mr. Brown, I don't know how you did it, but you've saved Jim's career."

"That's what I get paid for," said Blimey modestly enough. His mobile rang. It was Angie to say that she was overjoyed at the news. When the agent finished with the call, he saw that the other three were pouring over a fixture list, trying to work out exactly when Jim's ban would end. They finally agreed that the 25th of September would be the last day of his ban, the day they were due to play against Sheffield United.

"With a bit of luck Sky might take the game and it could be put back to the Sunday which would allow Jim to play," said Blimey.

"I doubt very much that he'd be selected," put in the manager.

"It's a long season and we'll need every player we've got," said the chairman. "I'm sure Jim will get a chance at some stage."

"I expect so," agreed the Manager reluctantly, hoping that injuries and suspensions would be kind to them.

Blimey left to sort out his page three stunner who was up the duff. Didn't he have any normal clients left?

"Don't call me for ten weeks," he told Razor, "do some serious training and lose some weight."

Talk between the Manager and the Chairman turned to the club's first match away at Manchester City and Jim realised he was no longer needed. He got up to leave.

"I hope you'll make all this up to us," said the Chairman.

"I intend to," replied Razor as he headed for the door.

"Don't be late for training on Monday," called out the Manager.

"Would I?" laughed Jim. The Manager didn't laugh.

Angie came down on the Saturday with Mikey. She had decided that it was time for Jim to get a place to live permanently. Razor couldn't see what was wrong with living in a hotel, but when Angie set her mind to something, she normally got her way. She'd rung round a few estate agents during the week and had selected five different properties for them to view, three in the morning and two in the afternoon.

"Where do I find the money to buy a place?" Jim wanted to know as they sat in a taxi en route for the estate agents.

"You don't. You're lucky that I know how to handle money. Blimey showed me some good investments a few years ago and I sold my mother's place last month as soon as I knew Mikey would need to live with you. I'll put my flat on the market when we get back to Manchester."

"You mean our flat?"

"No, I mean my flat. I got it in the divorce settlement remember?"

"But I paid for it."

"The only wages you ever earned that didn't get wasted on booze."

"I'm giving up," said Jim.

"You're right about that. I've fixed up for you to go to an AA meeting tonight in Greenwich."

"AA? You know I don't like cars." Angie didn't laugh at his joke.

"Get used to it Jim, you'll be going every night. It's the best way to keep you out of the pub."

"Shit!"

"And don't swear in front of the boy."

Razor looked across at his son who had earphones on listening to his music.

It wasn't until the afternoon that Angie saw somewhere she liked. It was a fairly new flat in the docklands overlooking the water with huge windows, light and airy with a spectacular view.

"This is the one," she whispered to Jim behind the agent's back.

"We can't afford this," hissed Razor.

"I can," decided Angie, "if I sell everything I've got. This is where I want Mikey to spend his school holidays. Just look at that view Jim, it's amazing."

Razor looked out of the window and across the water.

"It'll do, I guess."

"You just better make sure there's enough money to pay the bills every month, that's all I ask. Mikey needs somewhere to call home."

"Jim looked at his son, earphones firmly in place and wondered how on earth he was going to make this huge empty flat feel like a home. To make a home for Mikey would mean that Jim would have to become a father, and the thought scared him to death.

Jim saw his ex-wife and son off on the train from Euston on the Saturday night. Angie wanted to put her flat up for sale straight away. Once that was done, she would come back down south and start to search for a suitable boarding school for her son. She didn't particularly want her boy to board, but the other choice was having him live full-time with Razor, and he wasn't even capable of looking after himself, let alone another person as well. Could she imagine Jim waking up early in the morning, bathing and dressing Mikey, making his breakfast and getting him to school on time? Making his packed lunch every morning? No of course she couldn't. All Jim had ever had to do was get himself to training on time and kick a ball about for a couple of hours, and he had never even managed to do that very often. As she sat on the speeding train, looking out of the window as night fell, she found herself wondering what had attracted her to Jim Sharp in the first place. Perhaps they had been thrown together by circumstances. They had met just as both of them hit the height of their fame, and as soon as they had been seen together, the local press had made them into the year's dream couple. It had been fun for a while, the parties, the glamour, the excitement. Their wedding had been the social event of the summer in the North of England. But the bubble had soon burst.

The phone in Razor's room rang at nine o'clock Monday morning. It was Leonard.

"Get your arse out of bed Sharp, you're still a footballer and you've got training in an hour."

"Fuck off," said Jim, but after a few minutes of trying to pretend that he was still asleep, he realised that the damage was done and reluctantly stumbled out of bed. The minibar door hung open, gaping at him, and the tiny bottles of everything that it had contained lay scattered about the floor like beached silver fish. No wonder he felt like shit. But then, when didn't he feel like shit? Oh yes, when he was drinking, that was when he felt just about alive. It was the AA meeting that had done it, all that talk about booze had made him desperate for a drink and he had bolted out of the door the second he had been able to. He had caught a taxi back to the hotel. Locked himself in his room and drunk himself into oblivion. Oblivion was good. Oblivion was heaven. In oblivion he was still young and confident, he was still the best footballer in England. In oblivion he could forget about his ten week ban for punching a referee, he could forget that Angie was dying and he could forget that he was supposed to be some sort of father to a little boy he didn't even know. That he didn't even want to know.

Jim threw up after two laps of the training pitch, but it didn't make him feel any better. He kept going however, plodding doggedly along in last place, a steely determination written across his sweaty face. The Manager started the doggies without him and Jim trailed in well behind the others. He collapsed to the ground, gasping and wheezing like an old man on the verge of a heart attack, but it was the first time he had completed five laps of the pitch, and somewhere within his pounding brain he was pleased with himself. Okay some of the others had managed ten laps, but they were all ten years younger than him.

"Good AA meeting last night?" asked Leonard sitting down on the grass next to Razor after the doggies were finished.

"Worst night of my life," Razor replied honestly enough.

"They've got their work cut out with you, that's for sure."

"I only agreed to go to keep Angie off my back."

"There's no point in going if you're still going to get pissed up every night."

"They said that it can be a long process, there's no miracle cure. Going to your first meeting is a big step in the right direction though."

"Did you say I'm Razor Sharp and I'm an alcoholic?"

"Sure. And my last drink was ten minutes ago."

"You had a drink before going into an AA meeting?"

"Yeah, I needed one just to settle the nerves. I popped into a pub near Euston after seeing Angie off."

"Christ Jim, you're the pits."

151

"Tell me something Leonard. How can you go out every night for so long and not drink?"
"I don't need alcohol to have a good time."
"I need alcohol even to have a lousy time."
"You need to quit Jim, you need to save your career before it's too late."
"Career? What career?"
"Well, have you thought about life after football?"
"No."
"Then you need to keep playing for as long as possible, at least until you decide what you're going to do when you finish."
"And what are you going to do when you give up football?"
"I'm going to be the first black England manager."
"No big ambitions then?"
"You've got to have goals in life Razor."
"Goals are what I do for a living sonny boy," laughed Razor. "I was scoring goals before your old man started scoring with your mum. He struggled to get to his feet for the only bit of training he even remotely enjoyed, shooting practice. There was a young reserve defender along to help out, since the forwards were supposed to start from the half way line, outpace the defender and then beat the keeper.
"I can't beat that kid in a race from the half way line," complained Jim to the Manager.
"Well, you're going to have to try, that's the way I'm looking to play, the ball over the top for the forwards to chase."
"What? What happened to passing the ball into feet?"
"We've got to play to our strengths, and pace in attack is our strength."
"It's not my strength."
"You're not in my attack for the first seven games of the season, remember?"
Jim knew when to shut up and did so. He watched as Leonard chased onto through balls pumped over the top from the half way line. He was quick, there was no doubting that, he beat the young defender by a couple of yards every time, but once he had the ball within reach he struggled to control it, and by the time he had it properly under control

the goalkeeper was on him. It happened time and again as the Manager watched on in frustration.

"Okay Leonard, take a break. Let Jim have a go."

Jim looked at his Manager as if to say he was wasting his time, but walked onto the pitch all the same. Everyone knew Razor wasn't going to outsprint the young defender, it was just a ploy to give Leonard and the other two young forwards a bit more confidence seeing the legendary Razor Sharp fail to score.

The coach prepared to kick the ball over the top into the space for Jim to run into, and just as he did Razor elbowed the defender in the ribs and sent him sprawling. Jim jogged forward, saw the keeper approaching, and casually chipped the ball over him into the empty goal.

"That what you had in mind Boss?" asked Razor when he returned to the half way line.

Angie was back in a few days with Mikey, to start looking for his new boarding school. When he met them at Euston, Razor saw the first signs of Angie's illness on her face. Until then it had been as if nothing was wrong, outwardly at least. But now her cheekbones were sunken, her forehead creased with worry and she seemed suddenly small and fragile. Sure she had slapped on a ton of makeup to try to keep up the appearance of normality, but it wasn't enough to fool Jim. It was going to be horrible for little Mikey to watch his mother slowly die before his eyes.

Angie had rung several schools for information and had a bag full of brochures and letters. She didn't really want Mikey to be in London though, and thought that Sevenoaks might be the ideal place. They switched stations by tube and took a train into Kent to look around and see what Mikey thought. Jim's son sat by the window in the train gazing out at the fields as they left the dirty sprawl of the city behind. He was listening to his music.

"I want him to be at a school that's near enough for you to go see him sometimes," Angie whispered to her ex-husband.

"Sure," said Jim.

"Sevenoaks isn't far, you can get yourself a car and pop down at the weekends, at least until you start playing football again."

153

"I haven't driven a car in years," Jim told her, "not since I wrote off that Jag."

"Well, maybe you ought to get one. The flat at Docklands has got a reserved parking space and you could motor down to Sevenoaks quite easily on a Saturday or Sunday, whichever day you aren't playing."

"I don't know Angie..."

"Please Jim. You've got to look after Mikey. God I'm gonna miss him so much." She started to cry, softly so as not to let her son hear over the top of his discman. Jim put an arm around her shoulders and realised that underneath her beautiful clothes and eighties shoulder pads she was just skin and bone.

"Why did this have to happen to me?" sobbed Angie.

"You've still got to fight it kid," whispered Jim.

"I've been fighting so hard you can't imagine. I'm just tired now, so tired."

"Relax. Have a rest. Get your strength back a bit for when we get to Sevenoaks."

Mikey's CD finished the last track and he rummaged around in his bag for another one. He looked across and saw his mother, her eyes closed, resting her head upon his father's shoulder. His father also had his eyes closed, his head back against the dirty seat, silent tears meandering down his cheeks. Mikey would never have thought that Razor was capable of tears.

A few days after returning to Manchester, Angie was rushed into hospital. She couldn't stop vomiting and the doctor's put her on a drip to make sure her body was getting some nutrients since she couldn't keep any food down. Jim got the phone call after training and immediately headed for the train station to get there as soon as possible.

He found his ex-wife looking pale, ghostly-white, her face devoid of makeup seemed devoid of life. When he entered her room, she had her eyes closed and he thought for one horrible moment that she was dead. He approached the bed and touched her hand and her eyelids flickered open.

"Hi Jim," she gasped.

"I came as soon as I could," he told her. She nodded briefly and closed her eyes once more. Jim sat on a chair next to the bed and watched her resting. She seemed at peace, but Jim knew her mind was tormented by the thought of having to leave her son, and, worst of all, leaving her son to him. Maybe she would be able to keep an eye on things from up above, and yet Jim couldn't convince himself on that point. Was there life after death? Or was there just silence? Jim was terrified of silence. Terrified of that silence that followed your name being read out over the public address system before a match. That was the silence that meant that your career was over. At home games your name should be greeted by a hearty cheer, preferably louder than anyone else's, and at away grounds with deafening booing which showed that they feared you. But to be greeted by silence was the worst thing of all. And Jim was fast approaching silence.

The football season started without Jim. Athletic travelled to Manchester City for the first game and stole the three points in front of a hostile crowd of nearly 32,000. Jim watched it live on TV in Angie's hospital room, Leonard Molloy scoring the only goal of the game running onto a long through pass, just as they'd practiced in training.

SEVEN

Jim caught the last train back to London every night, trained the next day and returned to Manchester straight away to spend a few hours with Angie. He had asked for a few days off but he had been refused apparently he more than anyone needed every minute of training and so he became a long distance commuter. Razor hated travelling, he always had done, even when he was at United and they had played pre-season games in unfamiliar places, to him it was just a chore. In the end all he ever did was sleep or gaze absent-mindedly out of the window. He would take Mikey out for tea at a burger or pizza place and then take him back to Angie's friend who was looking after him short-term. Then he returned to the hospital always with the fear that he would arrive to be told that Angie had passed away. But Angie was determined to at least be well enough to take Mikey down to Sevenoaks for the start of the school year. It broke her heart to think of sending her boy to boarding school, but what else could she do?

Angie discharged herself from hospital towards the end of August in order to spend a few days with her son before taking him to Kent.

London Athletic's dream start to the season, beating the bookies' favourites for promotion on their own ground, was followed by a 1-0 home win over Wycombe Wanderers in the Worthington Cup, Malloy scoring from the penalty spot midway through the first half. He scored again in the first home league match on August 14th, but it was only enough for a draw with Portsmouth. Another 1-1 draw followed against London rivals QPR before the unthinkable happened and they were dumped out of the Worthington Cup, losing 4-2 in the return leg against Wycombe.

Jim took Mikey to the next game against Walsall whilst Angie rested back at the hotel. He was horrified to see his team mates lose 2-1 in a bad-tempered game. The bubble of instant promotion back to the top flight had well and truly burst. Still, there were a lot of games left to play, and at least their new signing, Leonard Malloy, had made a good start. He had already won over the crowd with his enthusiasm and electrifying pace. Razor wondered how he was ever going to win over the crowd, if he ever got to play of course.

The first weekend in September there was no game because of the international fixtures, and on the Sunday Angie and Jim travelled down to Sevenoaks with Mikey for the start of term. Razor knew that his ex-wife was making a supreme effort for the sake of her son, and every now and then, she would grimace as a spasm of pain racked her body. Jim was certain that he could never have been as brave as she was. It wasn't fair at all. Angie was genuinely a nice person and a mother, why did she have to get ill? And Jim who was a waster and an alcoholic and a good-for-nothing and certainly not a father, why was he in good health?

Mikey was sharing a room with another boy who was also new to the school and Angie was hopeful that the two of them would look after each other and become friends. Mikey was certainly going to need a friend.

When the time came to say goodbye, Angie broke down despite all her resolve and strength, and Jim had to drag her apart from Mikey and away from the school. They left the boy behind in tears. The housemaster, who was aware of the situation had promised to keep a close eye on things, but even so, it broke Angie's heart to leave her son behind. She cried all the way back to London on the train. Jim could imagine his poor little son crying himself to sleep that night in his new surroundings. Perhaps somewhere deep inside him there was a part of him that was a father after all. He vowed to himself to go to see his son as often as he could. Every weekend, either Saturday or Sunday when there wasn't a game on. God knew he had nothing else to do.

Back in London, Angie persuaded Jim to go to an AA meeting again and reluctantly he went along. She walked him to the door to make sure he didn't disappear to the pub on the way. Razor sat through the meeting as he sat through tactics briefings, letting it all go in through one ear and back out of the other. Sure he stood up to tell his story and was actually surprised to hear himself say that it had been two days since his last drink. He hadn't even noticed that he had gone so long without alcohol. What with meeting Angie and Mikey from the station , taking his son to the match and then the trip down to Sevenoaks, he had completely forgotten about booze.

The group listened in silence as he told them about his drunken prostitute mother, about how she never allowed him into the house and so he had had to spend his childhood out in the street playing football. He told them that when his mother had died he had had nowhere to go, and so he had climbed over a wall to get into Manchester United's training ground, persuaded the Youth Team Manager to let him play and the rest was history. He skipped the bit about being called up for England and scoring a goal for his country, although perhaps some of the other men there knew about that. He told the group about his injury and how frustration and boredom had thrown him into the welcoming arms of drink. He told them about his failed marriage and about the son he had hardly seen for eight years. He began to cry. He apologised immediately for his tears, but noticed that a few of the others were crying too, no doubt thinking about their own stories. Alcohol had been like a shroud over his life, and at last he wanted it lifted.

After the meeting, he and Angie went for a pizza and Jim drank a diet coke and they talked about the days when they had first been together and both realised that there had been some happy times too.

The next morning, Jim went to training and Angie returned to Manchester where she had an afternoon appointment at the hospital.

Jim was beginning to notice a difference in his body. The training, the afternoons swimming or doing weights with Leonard and his abstinence from alcohol were starting to make him feel better, he was losing weight too and getting quicker in the sprints. He had even signed up to Leonard's special diet that the hotel provided for him, and the two ate together and talked about football, since it was the only thing they could ever possibly have in common. Leonard was obsessed by one day playing for United and Razor would tell him what it was like on a day to day basis to be at one of the World's top clubs. After their evening meal, Jim would reluctantly head off for his AA meeting and Leonard would race off in his Porshe into Central London for a night out. Things had changed so much, that sometimes in the mornings it was Razor who telephoned Leonard's room to wake him for training. With his ban nearing an end, Jim was itching to play. The problem of course was that he still had to convince the manager that he was worth a place in the team. He hoped that his efforts in training hadn't gone unnoticed.

Angie would ring every evening to tell him how Mikey was doing and to remind Jim to attend his AA meeting. Razor even rang his son himself one time, but it had been a very brief call since he had had no idea what to say to the boy. He had ended up promising Mikey that he would go down with Angie at the weekend. So Jim found himself on the train to Sevenoaks on the Sunday, having watched his team lose a second successive home game the previous afternoon 1-0 to Huddersfield. Angie slept throughout the brief journey, her head resting on Razor's shoulder. He could see quite plainly that his ex-wife was wasting away from within. Despite the makeup and the new wig and her smartest clothes she looked like a skeleton. This might well be her last meeting with her son and she knew it. She had made Jim promise that when the final days came he was not to bring Mikey to visit her. She didn't want her little boy to see her dying, even though it would be awful to be without him.

It was an emotional few hours with Mikey, although Angie was quick to stifle her tears whenever they came. Jim felt decidedly awkward, but did his best to put on a brave face for his son's sake, it was all he could think to do. Angie told Mikey that for half term he would be able to stay in the new flat in Docklands with Jim. He wanted to know if she would be there too, and she promised him that she would.

When it was time to leave, Angie gave Mikey the briefest of hugs and turned away to start the long walk back to the station. Jim stood for a few seconds, face to face with his son and saw the tears in the boy's eyes. He felt a terrible lump in his throat. From somewhere deep inside Razor's DNA a parental instinct reached out and embraced Mikey, and then with a quick "see ya soon kid" he rushed off to catch up with his ex-wife.

Angie cried all the way back to London whilst Jim just stared out of the window. He had never felt an emotion as strong as the one that had made him reach out and hug Mikey to him, and he realised that he would have to try to be some sort of father to the boy even though it scared him to death. But it wasn't just for his son, it was for himself too, he could see that now.

After two home defeats, London Athletic travelled to Nottingham on Sunday 19th September for a live television appearance against one of the favourites for promotion. Jim travelled on the coach with the team as his ban was due to end the following Saturday. He wanted to show the Manager that he was keen to be involved as soon as possible. Forest, Jim's old club, had been relegated the previous season like Athletic, and were also desperate to return to the top flight at the first attempt. It was a passionate game, two big guns blazing away at each other for the nation to enjoy. Although Forest created the best chances, Athletic battled well and came a away with a creditable draw. The downside was a late injury to Leonard Malloy who seemed to have dislocated his shoulder after falling awkwardly. He was taken to hospital and didn't travel back with the team. Razor stayed on in Nottingham to make sure the big guy was being looked after and then took a train to Manchester to be with Angie.

He found his ex-wife looking drawn and ghostly, tired and wasted as he had never thought to see her. She was lying in bed when Jim arrived, the doctor fussing around her. It was quickly decided that she needed to go back into hospital. Razor went with her in the ambulance and held her tiny hand as she slipped in and out of consciousness.

At some stage during the night, Jim fell asleep too and when he awoke with a start he found himself alone in the dark with Angie. For a moment he thought she was dead, but eventually he was able to make out the faint sounds of her breathing. He knew that Angie was fighting for all she was worth, but it was a fight she had no chance of winning.

In the morning Jim rang the club and told them that he was going to stay at the hospital with Angie until the end. He was told that the game against Sheffield United had now been switched to the Sunday to be shown live on TV, which of course made him eligible to play. But football was the farthest thing from his mind at that moment.

Angie held on and held on, fought and fought, and died early on Monday morning. Jim awoke to hear a terrible rattle from her throat and then she was gone. He sat alone with her for a while, just holding her hand and whispering to her. He told her just how much he was going to miss her, how much he regretted how he had behaved towards her when they were married and how he wished that they could have their time together over again. He promised her that he would look after their son. He sat alone and cried for a while and then wearily got to his feet to look for a nurse.

When he had talked to a funeral director and made plans for Angie's cremation, Jim caught a train back down south to tell Mikey the bad news. He called Blimey from a phone box at the station, and for once the agent was dumbstruck.

Telling his son about Angie's death was the hardest thing Jim had ever done. He held Mikey tight as the boy's tiny body convulsed with huge sobs, rocking him gently as he had never done when he was a baby. They travelled up to Manchester on the train, Mikey listening to his music and occasionally crying silent tears. Razor was glad that the boy had earphones in since he wouldn't have known what to say to make the journey pass. In Manchester they checked into Jim's usual hotel and then went out for a burger. At a loss for what to do, Jim finally decided that they should go to the cinema, and for a couple of hours he sat in the darkness with his eyes closed as Mikey munched popcorn and watched some loud cartoon thing.

Angie's funeral, rushed as its preparation had been, was still well attended. Blimey had obviously been busy on the phone and there were a lot of minor celebrities and ex-footballers there, all of whom had known Angie in her heyday as a one-hit wonder pop star. Mikey stood in between Jim and Blimey squeezing their hands as tightly as he could, as his mother's coffin disappeared along a conveyor belt towards the blast furnace. As soon as it was over Blimey drove them back down to London. On the way they heard on the radio that London Athletic had been soundly beaten 3-0 by Sheffield and that the manager's job was on the line. It was funny, but Jim hadn't thought about football at all over the last few days. It didn't seem important anymore. Even the fact that he could play again didn't give him any hope.

When they reached the hotel in London there was a message waiting for Jim, telling him, he was in the squad for the match against Crystal Palace the next day and that there was a tactical briefing the following morning at ten o'clock and that he mustn't be late. He got Leonard to keep an eye on Mikey while he went to his AA meeting, his first in a while, but he needed to get Angie's death off his chest rather than drink himself into oblivion which was the other option.

London Athletic had now gone six league games without a win. Definitely not the sort of form to get them promoted back to the Premier League and the Manager knew that the next defeat would be his last. Possible big-name replacements were already being talked about in the press. The Manager hoped that a victory in a local derby would instantly get the fans back on his side and he was praying that his team would come good for him. Jim sat and listened impatiently as the tactical briefing raged around him. He'd heard it all before from stressed-out managers desperately trying to save their jobs. Some shouted at you, some begged you to find a little bit of extra talent that you'd never known you had, some threw things around, some just quietly pleaded with you, and most changed their tried and trusted tactics in a final throw of the dice.

Jim was glad that Leonard was around during the afternoon as he just wanted to lie on his bed, trying to get himself into some sort of frame of mind to play football again, after so long. He was only on the substitute's bench, but he suspected that if things weren't going well then the Manager's final forlorn hope would be to throw him on and trust that the legend of Razor Sharp still had one final glorious chapter to be written.

Jim got to the ground as late as he dared without risking the Manager blowing his top at him, but star strikers were meant to arrive late, that was what they did. Anyway, he hated watching other players going through their pre-match routines when he was just going to be sitting on the bench. A quarter of an hour before the start he went out for a kick about with the goalkeeper and was surprised to receive a small round of applause from the crowd. Poor bastards, he thought, they were so desperate for a win, that they were even polite to him, in the hope he might give them a goal. The Palace fans away at the other end of the ground ignored him, not even bothering to sing 'you fat bastard' or 'who ate all the pies' in his honour. They obviously didn't see him as any sort of threat and why should they?

When the teams ran out of the tunnel, it was to find the beautiful new Millennium Ground barely half full. The attendance was over nine thousand down on that of the first home game of the season, even though it was a local derby and for the first half, the stay-away fans must have been more than happy with their decision. Athletic were a shambles. Some of the players were nervous and made mistakes, others were trying too hard, and no one seemed relaxed enough to be able to pass the ball to feet. It was only the fact that Palace were going through a rebuilding phase and didn't have a very strong team that kept Athletic in the game. Palace wasted several golden opportunities, missed a penalty and only went in 1-0 up at the break. They should have had five or six.

The Athletic dressing room was like a morgue, the Manager a pale and ghostly shadow of his former self. He tried to go through the motions of geeing his players up, but it wasn't inspiring, his heart just didn't seem to be in it. No doubt he had already started to wonder just how far down the leagues he would have to go to get another job in football.

When they went out for the second half it was blowing a gale in from the Thames and pissing down with rain. The fans that had come must have been wishing that they were in the pub with their stay-away mates. The only thing they could think of to take their minds off the miserable weather and the even more miserable match was to chant for the board to sack the Manager over and over again. The Manager sat in the dugout, his face in his hands, his elbows on his knees as the minutes dragged by. With twenty minutes left he suddenly lifted his face and looked at Razor as if he'd just remembered that he had him there. It was time for the final throw of the dice, time to send in the forlorn hope. What did it matter now if Jim Sharp played? It might be his first and last league appearance for the club, a new manager might not want him involved at all.

Razor went through the motions of warming up along the touchline, did a few half-hearted stretches and then returned to the dugout. He got the nod from the Manager and stripped off his tracksuit ready to take the field. The Manager pulled off a defender.

"Where d'ya want me to play Boss?" asked Razor.

"Play where the fuck you like," came the Manager's reply and Jim ran onto the pitch to almost total silence. It seemed to rain even heavier than before, and Jim turned up the collar of his shirt and went up front to lead the line, it was the only thing he knew how to do. That he would get little or no service he was sure, but it was too cold to stand around waiting for a pass that might never come. And so he set about chasing lost causes and generally making a nuisance of himself across the Palace back four who'd had a pretty easy evening's work up until then.

The other Athletic players noticed Jim's efforts and began to respond and even some of the fans who had been making their way to the exits turned back to watch. Jim got his reward in the final few minutes as a defender slipped on the wet surface and presented Razor with a one on one against the Palace keeper. He fainted to shoot, sat the keeper on his arse and chipped the ball into the goal. It was possibly Athletic's first shot on target all game, but sometimes one was enough. Palace fizzed angrily for the final moments, but Athletic held on to snatch a point.

The Manager ranted and moaned in the changing room, told them that they hadn't deserved to get anything from the game and that if he had any money to spend he'd replace the lot of them. Jim was glad to see him bothered again, at least now he seemed like a man who was prepared to fight to keep his job rather than just lay down and die. Funny that it should be Razor who had given him back some hope. In the press conference after the game Jim dedicated his goal to Angie and promised the fans that there were plenty more to come. It had been a long time since a goal had brought him any pleasure, but this one had. Mikey was so excited at having seen Jim score that he talked about nothing else in the taxi all the way to the hotel. Razor had meant to take the boy back to school the following day, but maybe he would let the kid stick around for a while. He should get the keys to the flat soon and it would be nice for Mikey to choose a few things for his new bedroom.

The back pages of the newspapers carried Jim's picture the next day as there had been no Premier League fixtures, and there were headlines like 'still sharp' and Razor's a cut above the rest' and such like, the sort of headlines he had commanded on a weekly basis whilst at United. It was nice to make the sports pages for the right reasons for a change, and Jim allowed himself a contented smile as he lowered himself into the shallow end of the hotel swimming pool. Mikey sat on the edge dangling his feet in the water.

"What's it like to score a goal Jim?" asked the boy.

"It's a great feeling kid, but it don't last long. Goal scorers are always under pressure."

"Must be nice to have everyone cheering and shouting your name."

"Sure, but it's my job to score goals."

"Reckon you'll start in the next one?"

"Dunno, that's up to the Manager."

"Can I come again?"

"I've gotta take you back to school."

"Please Jim, can't I stay until the weekend?"

"Okay. We might get the keys to the flat before the weekend."

"Can I have bunk beds?"

"Course you can."

"Will Leonard look after me at the match again?"

"Sure I will little buddy," came Leonard's voice from behind them. He had taken the strapping off his shoulder and was holding it with his good arm.

"You be careful," Jim warned him.

"No worries man, I'm just gonna do fifty laps," replied Leonard as he eased himself into the warm water.

EIGHT

Jim and Mikey stood in the entrance hall of their new flat. Now that the previous owner had removed the minimalist furniture that had been there before it seemed huge. The lounge had windows from ceiling to floor with those fantastic views out across the water that Angie had loved. God it was a shame that she wasn't here to make the place into a home for their son. Jim knew fuck all about furniture and design and shit like that. Fortunately Leonard was coming over with a friend who would be able to help them out, he was a designer for a local furniture megastore. Mikey's bedroom was next to the lounge and had a view out across Docklands. It too had big windows and seemed like a huge empty cave with all the light at one end.

"Need a desk for school work," said the boy quietly.

"Sure kid, just tell Leonard's friend what you want. He'll see to it."

"And the bunk beds?"

"Sure."

The doorbell rang and Jim went to answer it. Leonard's friend had arrived with his arms full of catalogues for them to look at. It was going to be an expensive afternoon thought Jim gloomily. Luckily he had spoken to Blimey about the state of his finances and his agent had told him that as long as he didn't go overboard that there was plenty of money in his account to cover furniture. He advised Jim that he should start taking a more active interest in his own accounts which Razor promised to do. Maybe he could do a bookkeeping course or something. Who knows, it might even lead to a new career after football. Right! Who was he trying to kid? He couldn't trust himself with his own money, let alone someone else's.

On the Saturday, Jim took Mikey back to school. When he was walking back alone down the sloping high street towards the station, he realised that he was going to miss the boy. Still, he had an AA meeting that night and then he was in the squad for the Sunday game against West Brom. On Monday he was going to move into the flat. He had plenty of things to occupy his mind and keep it off drink. Shit, why had he just thought about drink? He tried to remember how long it had been since his last drink, but quickly tried to stop himself even thinking about it. He still couldn't trust himself, once an alcoholic always an alcoholic, but it had been a while. At the end of training he drank a couple of those isotonic sports drinks with Leonard and at other times it was diet coke or just water. He'd had the minibar removed from his room which had helped.

Physically he felt better than he had done for a long time, possibly even since he had been at United. He wondered if the Manager would put him in the starting line up after his goal in the previous match. He tried not to get his hopes up.

West Brom had had a poor start to the season and were in the relegation places. Both managers were under pressure to turn things around, and it was always going to be a cagey sort of game. Jim was forced to watch from the bench. He saw that his team mates were performing a little better than in the previous match although they still couldn't create any half decent chances.

The game rambled along, not really going anywhere, both teams reluctant to take any chances. The ground was silent for long spells as the crowd watched in growing disappointment. With twenty minutes or so remaining, West Brom managed to get the ball into the box and their centre forward collided with the Athletic keeper. The referee had a rush of blood to the head and pointed to the penalty spot. He then sent the keeper off. The crowd came instantly to life booing the referee for all they were worth. The substitute goalkeeper was quickly rushed on in place of a forward to face the spot kick. It took a while for everything to settle down and for the new keeper to get into position, but it didn't bother the West Brom player who had been waiting to take the penalty. He casually planted the ball in the bottom right hand corner and turned to milk the applause of the two thousand or so travelling fans cornered away on the far side of the ground.

If the Athletic Manager thought that things couldn't get any worse, he was wrong. Five minutes later the substitute keeper rushed out of his area to head away a through pass, realised that it was going to bounce over his head and instinctively stuck up a hand to stop it. The referee had no choice but to show another red card.

The Manager was going bananas on the touchline at the referee and Jim and the Physio had to drag him back to the dugout.

"Christ," fumed the Manager, "who the fuck's gonna go in goal now?"
"I'll do it," offered Jim.
"You? What d'you know about goalkeeping?"
"I used to play in goal in five-a-sides at United all the time."
"All right then, what the fuck. Just don't get sent off."
"Okay Boss."

Jim changed into the keeper's jersey and took his gloves and then ran onto the pitch amid howls of laughter from both sets of fans. The Manager had pulled off his last remaining forward since he didn't want it to become a cricket score in the fifteen minutes that were left of play. He had fifteen minutes in which to decide whether he should resign or wait to be sacked in the morning.

Razor took his place on the goal line behind the wall and waited for the free kick to be taken. The West Brom player struck the kick toward the top right hand corner of the goal. With surprising agility for such a big guy, Razor launched himself into the air, finger-tipping the ball around the post. The Athletic fans who had grouped behind his goal went wild with delight.

The corner came across and Jim leapt high in the air to claim it above the heads of his defenders. The crowd roared again. And so the game went on, Albion firing shots in from all angles, everyone thinking they had a chance to score. Jim pranced around the penalty area like a lion, brave, foolish at times, perhaps riding his luck, but certainly inspired and very entertaining. Whenever he had the ball safely in his hands he would kick it long and hard downfield in the hope of setting up an attack or at least to relieve a bit of the pressure.

With just a couple of minutes left, he caught the ball from a long shot and fired it quickly downfield. An Athletic player gave chase and forced a defender to put it behind for a corner. It would be the last throw of the dice. The crowd bayed for Jim to go forward and he set off up the pitch to arrive late and unmarked in the opposition penalty area. The ball swung in, hung briefly in the air midway between the penalty spot and the six yard line and Razor surged towards it. He sprang upwards, and powered an unstoppable header high into the roof of the net. For a moment there was silence as no one seemed to register what had happened, and then all of a sudden there was a roar that surly must have been heard all across London.

Monday morning, Jim picked up the keys to his flat and checked out of the hotel. It was somewhat sad to realise that his whole life fitted easily into two medium-sized suitcases and a large kitbag. Leonard was waiting in his car outside the hotel to drive Jim to Docklands.

"I'll go get the rest," he offered seeing Razor struggling with his two suitcases and the kitbag thrown over his shoulder.

"That's it."

"What?"

"This is all I've got."

"You're shitting me man!"

"No."

"Jesus, it'd take me weeks to move all my stuff. I've only been down here two months and I've bought enough new clothes to fill a lorry."

"Not really a big clothes person," mumbled Jim.

"I know that," laughed Leonard.

They reached the flat and sat on the floor waiting for the furniture to arrive. It came just before lunchtime, two fat blokes sweating and cursing as they carried things up the stairs. When they had gone the flat still looked empty. It was vast.

"Want some lunch," Jim offered Leonard.

"Please don't tell me you're gonna cook."

"Fuck no. I thought we could see what the local pub had to offer."

"Oh, in that case you're on. Not sure you need an introduction to the local pub though."

"Don't worry mate, all that drinking shit is behind me. I'm a changed man and I'm a goal scorer again."

"Don't get carried away. You've only got two."

"And you've only got three. Next game we'll be level."

"Think so?"

"I've been in the game long enough to know a lucky streak when I'm on one. I might get two next game if the Manager gives me more than ten minutes."

"We need to start winning if we're gonna get to the Premiership."
"We'll get a win soon, trust me."
"Wish I had your confidence."
"You will once we start playing together. Your pace and my finishing we could be a lethal weapon."
"Guess that makes you Mel Gibson then."
"Mel who?"

The week dragged by. They were back training on Tuesday. Jim continued to eat a light lunch at the hotel with Leonard, then they would have a swim or do some weights before Jim went to his new flat to fall asleep on the sofa. When he awoke he would head to the pub for his evening meal washed down with a couple of diet cokes before going to his nightly AA meeting. Jim had found a routine and he needed a routine.

On the Friday morning after training, the Manager announced his team for the following day's trip up to Bolton. Jim was rather annoyed to be told that he would be on the subs' bench again. As the players filed out at the end of the tactical briefing, the Manager came and put his arm around Razor's shoulders.

"Don't worry, you'll get on. We're only going with one up front so I expect whoever's up there to run himself into the ground for an hour and then have a change. Thought you'd prefer the shorter stint."

"Thanks Boss," mumbled Jim trying not to show how annoyed he was.

Razor sat towards the back of the coach on his own staring out of the window and daydreaming, letting the world outside pass him by as he always did when he had to travel. Had he dedicated his time on coaches and planes to reading books, he could have got through a fairly large library by the time he had reached thirty. But, of course, Jim wasn't a reading sort of person, he just preferred to sit and stare out of the window. Other players chatted, or played cards or listened to music or just slept, especially those with young children, but Jim just stared out of the window as the world flashed past. Even Leonard had given up trying to have conversations whilst they were travelling. It had been an early start from London and it was still dark and raining. United wouldn't have made this kind of a journey on match day. They would have gone the day before and stayed overnight in a decent hotel, but this wasn't United, and long distance coach journeys on match days were normal.

When they arrived in Bolton the rain clouds were even thicker and darker than when they had set off. By the time the match kicked off, a gale-force wind was howling straight across the ground making any sort of decent football impossible. Jim sat curled up under a blanket in the dugout and looked across at the small group of Athletic fans huddled together for protection on the far side of the ground, the rain slanting directly in at them. What a miserable way to waste your Saturday afternoon he thought, not to mention how much it had cost them to get there.

If the weather was bad then the game was atrocious. The pitch quickly became a sea of mud and the players slid around out of control and found the ball had been left behind in puddles whenever they tried to dribble with it. Razor wanted to close his eyes and pretend he was elsewhere, but if the Boss thought he had nodded off there would be hell to pay. He picked up a bottle of one of those funny energy drinks and drank the lot down in one go in the hope that it might contain something to keep him awake.

About half way through the first half, the Manager told all his subs to go out to warm up, he didn't want anyone dying of hypothermia or anything. Out of the relative shelter of the dugout Razor was punched and kicked by the strength of the wind, jeered at by the home supporters and dumped on by the rain which seemed to be doing its best to turn into sleet. This was the glamour side of football he told himself. If the weather didn't improve for the second half the referee might seriously have to start thinking about calling the game off.

In the warmth of the changing room during the break, those who had had the misfortune to have been playing sat wrapped up in blankets holding scalding cups of tea to try to thaw out their frozen hands. The Physio was gently removing waterlogged boots and frozen socks in the hope of getting some life back into the players' feet. No one bothered to speak and the only sound was the chattering of teeth. Eventually the Manager, his lips blue with cold, his hair flayed by the gale, stood up to tell them that they were doing well, that things were going according to plan and they just had to keep chasing everything.

"It's the only way to keep warm," muttered someone and there were nods of approval all around.

With half an hour to go in the game, the Manager kept to his word and Razor was put on up front on his own. He wasn't really a chasing around sort of guy, but he reckoned that if he stood still for too long his bollocks might turn into ice cubes. So, reluctantly, he jogged half-heartedly after the ball whenever it came near, making sure to keep his hands thrust under his armpits for warmth. Athletic had come for a draw, and any forward play was unintentional and uninspired. With ten minutes left Jim saw a defender getting a bit bogged down in a puddle and set off to hurry the man along. Suddenly, as he ran, he had an image flash into his mind of the defender trying to play the ball back to his keeper and the goalie slipping over as he went to kick clear. Ignoring the defender, Razor ran straight towards the goal, and sure enough, it happened just as he had envisaged. The keeper slipped as he was attempting to clear and fell over, and Jim found himself with an open goal. For a second he went into a state of total shock, but then his instincts took over and he belted the ball as hard as he could into the face of the gale and it smashed into the back of the net sending a million water droplets crashing to the ground. Razor stood still, unable to believe what had happened. He had scored a lot of goals in his career, but he had never had a vision of how to score one just before doing so. Perhaps all great goalscorers had these deja vu moments that allowed them to be in the right place at the right time. Maybe he had been denied them because of all the alcohol numbing his brain. Weird as fuck that was what it was. His team mates suddenly arrived en masse knocking him over onto the sodden ground, and they all piled on top of him in the mud. By the time he got to his feet, he was soaked to the skin and utterly miserable. The wind now seemed to blow right through him. The remaining few minutes were the longest of his life as he stood alone on the half way line watching his defence hold out for dear life against the obvious Bolton onslaught and the terrible weather conditions.

It wasn't until they were an hour out of Bolton on the coach the Jim finally stopped shivering and they were approaching the Midlands before he was able to feel movement in his feet again. He stared out of the window watching the night flash past and eventually fell into a troubled sleep.

The next day, Jim bought the Sunday paper at the station before boarding the train for Sevenoaks to go to see his son. It would be half term soon and Razor wanted to tell his son that his room was ready and waiting for him. He looked through the back pages of the newspaper until he found a single paragraph report on the previous day's match. It said simply enough that the weather ruined the game and that a slip by the Bolton keeper gifted a goal to ex-United striker Jim 'Razor' Sharp, his third goal in as many games. It wasn't much but Jim was satisfied. He felt that there were more important reports to come. If he really had developed some sort of sixth sense about when a goal was in the offing, then he might go on to get thirty by the end of the season. He'd always dreamed of having a thirty-goal season. The closest he had ever come had been twenty-five in 1987-88 when United had finished as league runners-up behind Liverpool. Maybe this could be his season. Was he too old for an England recall he wondered.

Jim just got back into London in time to get to his AA meeting. Sunday nights always got a hundred percent turnout as everyone went along to avoid the temptation of reaching for the scotch when faced with the prospect of Monday morning looming ever closer.

A few minutes after the meeting had got underway, a new woman came in, shaking her umbrella and flustered at having arrived late.

"I'm so sorry," she said several times. She hung up her coat and left her umbrella at the back of the room and then pulled over a chair to join the group. Jim moved his chair aside a bit to allow her to slot into their circle. She smiled a quick thank you. Razor thought that her face looked tired and her eyes were a little red maybe from lack of sleep, but her smile was nice enough.

The new woman was asked to tell her story as all newcomers were, and quietly, shaking a little with nerves, she told the group how a hit and run driver had killed her little boy. He had been playing in the street in front of her house. He said she just hadn't been able to cope and after a nervous breakdown she had turned to drink which had eventually cost her both her job and her marriage. By the time she had finished her story, she was in tears, but she ended by saying that she had been dry for nearly two months and was starting to get her life back on track. She had moved to the area the previous week to start a new job and so had been forced to change AA groups.

Jim suddenly felt incredibly selfish. This woman had turned to booze for comfort after the death of her child where as he had used it to destroy himself for no good reason. There had been a time, which seemed like a long time ago now, when he had had everything. How many schoolboys dreamt of becoming professional footballers? Millions. How many actually achieved that dream? Just a lucky handful and of those lucky few, how many went on to wear the famous red shirt of Manchester United? How many knew what it was like to hear a packed Old Trafford chanting your name? Jim knew now that he was one of a privileged few, and he knew that at just twenty-three he had pressed the self-destruct button. Sure it was easy to blame everything on his injury, but there were players who'd had the same injury as him or even worse and had come back to be just as good as they had been before. Razor had never been a shadow of his former self, but it wasn't the injury's fault. By the time he was able to play again, he had put on a lot of weight, started to drink heavily and, worst of all, had a change of mentality that meant that he no longer appreciated his career and somehow felt compelled to destroy himself. The downward spiral had been a long one. United had been more than patient with him and given him chance after chance to prove himself, but he had been happy just to let his talent slowly ebb away. Until, one day, he wasn't good enough anymore and United wanted rid of him.

It was getting towards the end of the meeting when Jim was asked how things were going for him.

"Not so bad," he mumbled. He didn't really enjoy pouring out his heart to these people. Being famous had made him cautious about talking about his personal life in public. He always worried that someone would go running to a newspaper with Jim Sharp said this and Jim Sharp said that, but, well, if he was honest the newspapers probably didn't give a fuck about him now.

"When did you last see your son?" asked the group monitor.

"This morning. We had lunch and went for a walk in the park."

"That's good."

"It's gonna be half term soon. He's gonna come and stay. I dunno what to do?"

"Just be yourself," said the new woman whose name Jim couldn't remember, he was terrible at remembering things.

"It's just that I don't really know the boy. He's just come back into my life after my ex-wife's death. I've not been a father to him."

"Now's your chance to make up for lost time. Having a child is the most wonderful thing there is," and the woman began to sob again and Jim felt like shit. This woman had lost her kid and here was Jim worrying about whether or not he was capable of being a father to a little boy who needed him.

NINE

Friday morning's light training session ended with the usual pre-match team meeting. The following day's match was against Barnsley, one of Jim's former clubs, not that that meant anything to him. Malloy had been back in training throughout the week and had looked hungry to get his place back in the team, and Jim was worried that he might have lost his chance to make the starting eleven. Then, to his complete surprise, the Manager announced that they would play a four-four-two formation with him and Leonard starting up front together for the first time. It was important to build upon their win against Bolton.

When Razor's name was read out over the tannoy it was greeted by a polite cheer, but Malloy's name was greeted by a loud and enthusiastic roar, he had already become the crowd's favourite. Jim shrugged to himself and decided not to give a shit. Crowds were fickle things, you were a hero one day and an embarrassment the next, he knew that well enough. The game kicked off in weak afternoon sunshine before a crowd of just 14,000.

Jim meandered through the first half an hour, content to let Malloy do all the work. Chasing lost causes and tackling back were not a big part of his game, never had been, but they were things that the crowd liked to see. Leonard's efforts were cheered heartily. He was clearly enjoying himself and wanted to run for everything. Then, a long ball was played through for Malloy to chase and he easily outpaced the covering defender to find himself one on one against the keeper. Razor had followed in behind, as any good strike partner would, but he couldn't match Leonard's blistering pace. Faced with having to beat the keeper Malloy seemed to freeze and the goalie lunged for the ball which squirmed out to the edge of the box straight into Jim's path. He didn't hesitate to lift the ball up over the keeper, the last defender and his strike partner. It bounced on the line and fell into the net. God Jim loved this game. Athletic extended their lead early in the second half from a corner and the three points were in the bag. It was their first home league win of the season.

Straight after the game, Leonard drove Jim down to Kent to pick up Mikey for half term. As the driver battled through the traffic his passenger dozed in the seat beside him as if he didn't have a care in the world. When they arrived Mikey greeted his father with a quick smile and then climbed into the back of the car his discman in hand for the journey.

When Mikey fell asleep in the top bunk of his new bunk beds, Jim lay down on the couch to watch an old western, reluctant to go to his own bed in case his son should have a nightmare or something. He wasn't sure how he would react if the boy did start screaming or anything, but he thought it better to be ready. In the end, he awoke with a start at four in the morning and crawled into bed fully clothed. It reminded him of when he had been drinking.

Mikey went along to training on the Monday morning. It was only a light session as they had a game the following evening against Fulham. Afterwards, Jim took his son for a burger and then they rented some films and the father dozed on the sofa as the boy sat on the carpet staring at the TV screen. That evening, after a meal at the pub, Leonard came to look after Mikey so that Razor could go to his AA meeting.

Once again, the new woman arrived late, flustered and full of apologies. She eventually settled into a seat next to Jim and gave him a quick smile.

"How's it going with your son?" she whispered as the meeting resumed after her interruption.

"Okay, thanks," mumbled Razor and then they both turned their attention to the group.

At the end of the session, Jim made a beeline for the door determined to be first out as always. Outside it was raining, not that heavily, but just enough to be annoying, especially if you hadn't thought to bring a coat, as Jim hadn't. He hurried to the bus stop to wait in the shelter. If a bus came he would take it, if it stopped raining he would walk, it was only two stops. It was amazing that he actually preferred walking these days to catching the bus or taking a taxi. He'd never felt better really. His body was gradually slimming back into shape and his mind was certainly more active these days. A car pulled up alongside the bus shelter and when the window wound down he saw it was the woman from the meeting. Wendy, her name was Wendy, good one brain he thought.

"Want a lift?" she offered.

"No, thanks, I'm fine."

"Get in, there won't be a bus for ages at this time of night. You haven't even got a jacket."

Reluctantly Jim climbed into her small Peugeot and they set off. Her car was warm and Razor watched the raindrops falling through the headlight beams as they drove.

"Where do you live?" asked the Woman.

"Docklands," replied Jim, "it's not far."

"Just tell me when to turn," she said.

When they reached Jim's street, Wendy pulled the car over and looked across at her passenger.

"Thanks," mumbled Jim.

"Don't say much, do you?" she laughed.

"I'm not good at conversation."

"Guess not. What're you doing tomorrow? With your son I mean."

"Oh, nothin' special. Nothin' really."

"How 'bout we take him to the zoo? Think he'd like that?"

"Dunno. Dunno what he likes."

"All kids love the zoo," she assured him. "Shall I pick you up here at ten?"

"I've gotta team meeting at ten. We've gotta match tomorrow night."

"A match? What are you?"

"You don't know?"

"No, you've never mentioned it at the meetings I've been to. You only talk about your son."

"I play football."

"Really? Are you famous or something?"

"I guess."

"Who d'you play for?"

"Atheltic. That's how come I live round here."

"My ex-husband supports them."

"Yeah?"

"Goes every week. Used to drive me mad. My son had all the kit too..." suddenly she stopped at the mention of her child. Jim quickly racked his brain for something to say to change the subject.

"Listen, er Wendy, we can go to the zoo after my meeting. We can take a cab."

"A cab'll cost a fortune. We can go on the tube."

"Sure it'll be fun." They arranged to meet at the tube station and she drove off. Jim went up to the flat to see how Leonard and Mikey were doing. He found them playing on a games console that Malloy must have brought with him.

"Good meeting?" called out Leonard without taking his eyes off the TV screen where Mikey was dribbling a little computer footballer at will through Leonard's defence.

"Fine," said Jim. "Taking you to the zoo tomorrow Mikey."

"Goal!" shouted the boy punching the air in delight as the little computer footballer launched into a funny dance routine.

"The zoo?" asked Leonard, "want me to take you?"

"Uh, it's al'right, we're going with someone already."

"Yeah? Anyone I know."

"Someone from AA."

"I see. Man or woman?"

"Does it matter?"

"Razor you old rascal, it's a woman!"

"Just going to the zoo."

"Okay. Well, I'd better be off man."

"You can't go yet, I've only scored five this time," said the boy.

"Play against your dad. He's a footballer an' all."

"You gonna play Jim? Please."

"It's Leonard's toy, he'll wanna take it with him."

"You guys keep it for the holiday."

"Cheers," growled Razor.

"No worries. See you tomorrow."

Jim was pleased to hear at the team meeting that he would be starting up front with Leonard at Fulham. As soon as he could he was away with Mikey who had been sitting in reception listening to music. Wendy was

179

at the tube station waiting for them and Razor introduced her to his son. She gave the boy a quick kiss, much to his embarrassment and then Jim bought tickets and they got on the train.

The tube rattled along noisily enough to make conversation difficult and Jim was glad of that. Wendy was sitting next to Mikey and trying to grill him about school and stuff, so Razor stared out of the window as London rumbled by. It wasn't his city and he had no affection for it. It just didn't feel like home, even though he had a place of his own for the first time in years. He doubted that London would ever feel like home. It was too big, too unfriendly, too Southern. Jim didn't make plans for the future it was something he had never done, but it occurred to him that when his two years with Athletic were up and he found himself on the football scrap heap, he could sell the flat and move back up North. He could rent somewhere cheap, using the money from the flat to live off, while he set about drinking himself to death. If he'd been seriously into plans then it would have been a good one. Then he looked across at Mikey who for once was having a conversation with someone rather than listening to music and he realized that he couldn't sell the kid's home. He'd been a total bastard to the boy's mother, and it was too late to put things right with her, but at least he could try to do the right thing for their child. The thing that was killing him was what the fuck could he do after football? Maybe he'd pick Leonard's brains on that one sometime.

They reached the entrance to the zoo having strolled through the park. They looked at monkeys and gorillas. Mikey seemed happy enough. They found the café near the elephants and sat down to have lunch. Afterwards, they saw the lions and tigers and then the giraffes. Jim told Wendy that he needed to head back as he had to be at the ground to get on the team bus to Fulham.

"What's Mikey gonna do while you're with the team?" asked Wendy.

"He's coming with us on the bus, I've cleared it with the Manager. I'll get one of the player's wives to look after him during the game."

"Want me to look after him?"

"No. I wouldn't wanna put you out."

"I've never been to a football match, maybe I should see what all the fuss is about."

"Well, if you're sure."

"Tell you what, I'll take him for a burger or something before the match."

"Okay. We're having a light tea at some hotel near the ground. I'm sure he'd prefer a burger."

"How do I get to the ground?"

Jim was sure that his son would be happier with Wendy for a few hours than stuck with a bunch of farting footballers. She seemed really nice. Why on earth she wanted to waste her time with him he couldn't even begin to understand. Razor took his seat on the team bus and closed his eyes. They weren't going far, just hugging the river to Fulham, but even Jim's limited knowledge of London told him that it wasn't going to be an easy journey in the rush hour. He wanted to get a bit of sleep and relax a little, he felt tired from walking around the zoo. Not that he planned on doing much running during the match, god forbid. When they reached Craven Cottage, Jim got some tickets from the Manager and left them in the club office, just as he had told Wendy he would.

The match kicked off at a furious pace, as befitted a London derby, but it was Fulham who dominated in front of their own fans. After half an hour Razor couldn't remember whether or not he had actually touched the ball. Leonard his supposed strike partner had gone AWOL into midfield to try to get involved in some way. Eventually a ball was played forwards and Jim managed to get to it first. The defender marking Razor was a young lad, tall and lanky, and he tried to muscle Jim off the ball. Those were the wrong tactics and Razor shrugged him aside with a twitch of his powerful upper body. Then he surged into the box with just the keeper to beat. He neatly flicked the ball over the goalie's dive and just as he was about to roll the ball into the empty net the Fulham right back charged across and clattered him to the ground. Jim hit the ground like a sack of potatoes.

"Goal kick," shouted the referee.

"You out of your bloody mind?" asked Razor.

"You'd lost control of the ball."

"Rubbish, that's one of the most blatant penalties you'll ever see."

"I've made my decision," the ref turned to walk away.

181

"Fucking nonsense," mumbled Jim.

"What did you say?" asked the ref turning back towards him. "Okay, you're booked."

"What for?"

"For calling me fucking useless."

"You are fucking useless, but that's not what I said." The ref didn't care and wrote Jim's number on his yellow card before flashing it in his face.

"Fucking referees," mumbled Razor.

In the second half with the wind at their backs, Athletic began to enjoy a bit more possession. Leonard returned to the front line to help out and they managed to create a few half chances, all of which fell to Malloy and all of which he wasted. Jim was getting frustrated, all he needed was one half decent opportunity and he would put the game to rest. At last the moment came. Malloy slipped the ball through to him on the edge of the box and he wriggled free of his marker and pulled his leg back to shoot. Without warning his standing leg was knocked from under him and he crashed to the ground. This time it had to be a penalty.

"Free kick," shouted the ref. Razor picked himself up and looked to see where he was. He was a good yard inside the penalty area.

"You've gotta be joking," he shouted.

"Just outside," said the ref nervously fingering his top pocket. In the nick of time Jim remembered that Mikey was watching. The last game that he had seen had ended in utter disgrace for his father and somehow Razor managed to control himself and walk away. Inside though he was seething. The Manager reacted by substituting him immediately.

"I had it under control Boss," mumbled Jim as he walked past the dugout on his way to the tunnel.

"Just in case Razor. Just in case."

Jim showered and changed into a tracksuit and then went to stand in the tunnel so that he could watch the last few minutes of what looked like being a goal-less draw. The referee had other ideas though, and in the final seconds when Leonard slipped over in the box trying to get a late shot in on target, he blew for a penalty. The Fulham players couldn't believe it, neither could Razor.

Leonard scored from the spot, and Athletic had an unlikely third straight win. At last they were beginning to climb up the table, and their next two games were both at home against struggling opposition.

TEN

Jim and Leonard began to form a useful partnership over the following few weeks. In the next game against Port Vale they scored one each in a 2-2 draw. In the midweek game against Sheffield United Jim led the line superbly and set up Malloy for the only goal of the game. Razor got a late one away at Wolves at the end of October and then scored a hat-trick in a 3-0 home win against Grimsby Town. It was his first hat-trick in years and he strode off the pitch proudly clutching the match ball. He gave it to Mikey when he went to see him the next day.

It was Wendy who drove Jim to Sevenoaks to see his son. She was becoming a bit of a fixture in his life. She now picked him up every evening to take him to their AA meeting and dropped him home again afterwards. Sometimes she would park her car and go up for a coffee and they would chat for a while. Yes, she was definitely becoming a good friend. Jim had never had a female friend before.

Just when things seemed to be going well for Razor, he pulled his calf muscle late in the game against Swindon Town and had to limp off. He guessed that it was his body reminding him not to get too carried away. It meant he would have to sit out the next couple of games.

He was awoken early the following morning by the mad ringing of the telephone. It was Leonard Malloy.

"Christ, I'm in big trouble man," gasped Leonard, "I didn't know who to turn to."

"Trouble's my middle name," laughed Razor, "you name it I've done it."

"I was at a nightclub last night and I got photographed."

"That it? Jesus mate, you rang me up for that. It's Sunday fuckin' mornin'."

"I was kissing someone. I didn't realised there was a photographer there."

"So what. There's nothing wrong with kissing some bird is there? You haven't got a no kissing clause in your contract have you?" Jim laughed at his own joke, despite the early hour.

"It was a gay club man."

There was a silence.

"Razor? Are you there?"
"So that's where you go every night, gay clubs."
"Yeah."
"You could've told me."
"Does it make a difference?"
"No, of course not. I just thought we were friends that's all."
"We are friends. That's why I'm calling you now. It's in all the papers."
"Have you called your agent?"
"I don't have an agent."
"Okay, then we'll call mine. He'll know what to do, always does. Get your arse round here, make sure you're not followed."
"Cheers man, be there in ten."

Razor quickly got dressed and then called Bill Brown. Blimey was in bed, cuddled up to a page three stunner who he had taken out the previous night to help her celebrate her nineteenth birthday. She was half his age. He was just planning out in his mind how they were going to spend a long lazy Sunday. Sex of course, when she finally woke up. Breakfast at the local café and then back to his flat for some more sex. A walk down by the river followed by Sunday lunch. Some more sex. Watch the football on Sky. More sex. A few drinks down the local and then back to bed. She'd leave first thing Monday morning and he would probably never get another opportunity to shag someone like her again. He was determined to make the most of it. His phone rang. A little voice inside his head said don't answer it, but Blimey knew that his elite list of clients expected him to be on call 24 hours a day. Just as long as it wasn't Jim bloody Sharp he ought to be able to sort it out over the phone, besides, if he spoke loudly enough he might wake up sleeping beauty and get his sex-filled day under way at last. He answered the phone.

"Bill Brown."
"Blimey, hey it's Razor."
"Oh fuck."
"What d'you mean oh fuck?"
"What 'ave you done this time?"
"It's not me this time. It's Leonard my strike partner."
"Is he a client of mine?"
"No, you know he isn't."

"Well, thanks for ringing, nice to talk to you and all that, bye."

"Wait, wait. He's in a spot of bother and needs your help."

"Tell 'im to call his agent, not yours'."

"He hasn't got an agent, that's why I called you."

"I don't need another client like you."

"He isn't like me. He's sober and conscientious and talented. He's going all the way. He's the only strike partner I've ever had who's better than me."

"Really? Better then you when you were younger?"

"Yeah. This guy's got pace. Real pace. Could be your next England client. He won't be at Athletic very long. Imagine your fee when he moves to Chelsea or Arsenal."

"Sure he's that good?"

"Positive. He's just come up from the lower leagues and is a bit innocent round the edges, but don't worry, I'm gonna teach him everythin' I know."

"Blimey! That ain't gonna help 'im."

"Please Bill, help him out will ya. You'll get a superstar I promise you."

"What's he done?"

"He was photographed kissing a bloke in a gay club. It's in the papers this morning."

Bill Brown looked at his snoring nineteen year old and wondered how long she could possibly sleep for. Was it true that teenagers needed more sleep than adults? Maybe he could make a quick trip to Docklands and get this guy signed on. If he was really as good as Razor said, then he could be worth a fortune over the coming years. Blimey liked sex as much as the next man, but he liked money more. Besides, it was Sunday morning and there wouldn't be much traffic around. Maybe he could shoot over to Jim's place and get back in time for a pre-lunch blow job or something.

"Okay Jim. I'll come."

"Leonard's on his way over."

"See you in a bit."

Blimey scrambled for some clothes, wrote a quick note for Jessica Sleepyhead and left.

Leonard arrived at Razor's flat.

"What have I done?" he whined as Jim let him in.

"Easy big guy, Blimey's on the way. He'll sort it out."

"I dunno what I was thinking man. How could I be so stupid? How am I gonna face the rest of the team? How am I gonna face my family?"

"Your family don't know?"

"Never told anyone."

"Not even your parents?"

"Especially not my parents. My father's a minister of the church. It's gonna kill him."

Jim sat his friend down on a high stool at the American-style breakfast bar in the kitchen and set about making coffee. It was the one thing he was good at. Coffee and alcoholism went hand in hand. He left the coffee brewing and went to get the phone from the lounge.

"Here mate, call your mum. It's better if she hears it from you than reads it in the papers."

"What do I say?"

"Try the truth."

Jim left Leonard alone in the kitchen and went to tidy up the lounge ready for the visit of his agent. At least for once he wouldn't be on the receiving end of Blimey's bad temper. There were empty crisp packets, some half-drunk cans of diet coke and a couple of pizza boxes but it wasn't too bad. He noted with pride that there were no empty beer cans or whisky bottles to collect. He'd been sober for quite a while and he really felt better that ever. The headaches were gone, the stomach cramps, the permanent anger and the self-hatred had disappeared too. He was a man at peace with himself for the first time in as long as he could remember.

When he returned to the kitchen with his small collection of rubbish, he found Leonard sobbing down the phone to his mother. Quietly Razor binned his trash and poured the coffee.

Bill Brown arrived, businesslike and self-confident as always. He handed Leonard what he called a standard pre-contract agreement for him to sign.

"So, what's the plan?" asked Jim.

"Lie low. He should stay here with you for a few days until this blows over. I'll call the club and get him excused from training for a couple of days and then he'll have to face the music. Can't hide forever."

"That's it?" asked Leonard.

"That's it. Your private life is your affair. Blimey, you're not the first gay footballer for god's sake. Half my clients are gay."

"Okay man," responded Leonard, his face suddenly looking a little less troubled. Blimey left as quickly as he could in order to get back to, god what was her name? Melissa was it? Something like that.

The plan worked well. By the time the next match came around no one was interested in Leonard Malloy's sexuality anymore. Even the Ipswich fans didn't bother to taunt him. They were too busy urging their team forwards in the search for a victory that would keep them up near the top of the table. They got it too, a 1-0 win despite the non-stop efforts of Malloy playing upfront on his own whilst Jim watched from the stands. Another 1-0 defeat followed away at Tranmere Rovers. Things weren't looking so good, especially since their next game was against leaders Manchester City.

Jim was back in training. Light training, since it was all he knew, but he was aware that the Manager was keen for him to be back playing. Leonard upfront on his own hadn't worked, he needed Razor there to help him.

Match day was cold and windy at the new ground by the river. City played like league-leaders for the first half, neat passes full of confidence. Athletic chased shadows. Jim watched frustrated, hands on hips from the half way line. Things suddenly changed after the break however when the City captain had a rush of blood to the head and got himself red-carded for a tackle that put Athletic's right back onto a stretcher. Suddenly, the home team began to enjoy more possession and Razor scored a sitter from close range put on a plate for him by Malloy. He got a second, heading in from a corner and went off to protect his calf amid rapturous applause. Leonard scored a third goal before City got a late consolation.

Athletic were soon brought back down to earth on the Wednesday night with a defeat away at Crewe. Their last game before Christmas was at home to Birmingham and a bumper holiday crowd of almost 20,000 turned up to watch. Razor sent them home happy grabbing the winner in a closely fought 2-1 victory.

For Christmas Day, Jim decided to invite Leonard and Wendy round to join him and Mikey. Leonard was avoiding his parents and Wendy had no family to go to. She was invited on the strict understanding that she would do the cooking and not Jim. But they went shopping together in the local Sainsbury's with Mikey to get all the right stuff. Razor pushed the trolley whilst Wendy selected the ingredients. It was going to be the full works, turkey, sprouts, pudding, crackers, the lot. It was the first time that Jim could remember feeling excited about Christmas. He and Mikey had even decorated a tree with tinsel and flashing lights. There were several neatly wrapped presents underneath for Mikey. There was also a gift for Wendy that Leonard had helped Jim choose and there was one for Leonard that Wendy had helped him with.

Their Christmas dinner was a huge success although there was plenty left over as neither Jim nor Leonard wanted to eat too much with the Boxing Day trip to Stockport ahead of them in the morning. They toasted each other's health with cranberry juice. Mikey opened his presents after they had finished with the Christmas pudding. They were predictably electronic gadgets and CDs. Then they sat and dozed on Jim's beautiful big sofa and pretended to watch a Fools and Horses special.

Leonard left early and Jim went to tuck Mikey up in bed. It had been a long day as he had been up especially early to open the presents left in his Santa sack.

"Night son," said Jim as he paused at Mikey's door to turn out the light.

"Night dad," replied the boy sleepily. Jim flicked off the light but stood rooted to the spot in the darkness. He was in a state of shock. It was the first time the boy had ever called him dad. Jim felt a huge lump in his throat. When he regained his senses he hurried back to the lounge where Wendy was still sitting on the sofa.

"I ought to get going," she said, "if I'm to be back in the morning to look after Mikey."

"You can stay a bit longer if you like. We can watch a film or something."

Wendy laughed quietly.

"What's funny?" asked Jim.

"I thought you were going to ask me to stay the night."

"No Wendy, I wouldn't ...," mumbled Jim floundering for words.

"Can I ask you something?" she said.

"Sure."

"Why have you never tried to kiss me?"

"Because I wouldn't want to mess up our friendship."

"Who says it would mess it up?"

"I don't know. You've been so nice to me. I didn't wanna risk losing you. I never had a female friend before."

"So, that's it then? You just think of me as a friend?"

Jim was suddenly all confused. He looked at her for help.

"You can kiss me Jim, if you want to."

"I'm not sure I know how," he whispered. She moved her face closer to his, their lips almost touching.

"Give it a try," she told him.

BLUE-SKINNED GODS

ONE

My father hurried me along by the hand, tugging my arm so hard that I thought it might pull out from the shoulder. We were late. It was the first game of the season for his new team and we were late. I was thrilled that he was taking me with him, but not thrilled at having to get up early on a Sunday morning. I'd hidden under the duvet until he'd lost all patience and threatened to leave me behind and only then I'd tumbled out of bed and into my clothes which were conveniently on the floor where I'd left them. This wasn't like mum's house, where my clothes miraculously hung themselves up in the wardrobe during the night, no, this was dad's tiny house with its small rooms and uncomfortable camp bed, pizza boxes and empty beer cans. There was a different smell too. Mum's house was sickly sweet and perfumed, dad's was musky and stale.

At the end of the road a coach was waiting outside the pub. The first game of the season was away from home, hence the early start. We were the last to arrive, everyone else was seated already and as we climbed the steps a chorus of moans and groans greeted us. My dad found a double seat and sat down next to the window. The bus hadn't even turned right at the church when I heard his first snore. I don't know how he did it, but my dad could sleep anywhere. He said it was a result of a tiredness that he had accumulated owing to so many sleepless nights when I was a baby, but mum had told me that that was a load of rubbish. More than likely, it was what he had always done when travelling to a game. This team was minor leagues, but my dad had once been a professional player and travelled all over the country to play matches.

He hadn't been famous or anything, more of a bit part player in the lower divisions, but by sheer determination and a bit of luck he had more or less made a career out of football. His one moment of near greatness had come at the end of the 1992-93 season. He had come on as a substitute for Gillingham in the final league game against Halifax and scored two late goals to ensure the club didn't drop down into the conference. Halifax went down instead. My father's reward had come a week later when the Manager called him into his office and told him, with great regret, that his services would no longer be required by the club. My dad had been thirty-two years old and knew that no other league club would touch him. His finest hour on a professional football pitch had also been his last.

The bottom had dropped out of his world. He had absolutely no idea what to do with the rest of his life. He signed for non-league Gravesend and Northfleet so that he could at least keep playing, but his heart was no longer in it. A downward spiral began that saw him play for Chatham Town and finally Sittingbourne and then he gave up. He couldn't hold down a job and took to drinking heavily and so my mum left him. Following that, he disappeared from my life for a couple of years.

Then, quite unexpectedly he was back. He had cleaned up his act, stopped feeling sorry for himself and trained to be a PE teacher. He had got into football quite late and therefore he had finished his university degree before he signed for Brentford. Therefore, it only took him a year to qualify as a teacher when he finally decided to do it. He had got a job at a secondary school in Sittingbourne which was where my mother and I lived. We had sort of been abandoned there by his faltering career. He rented a damp little cottage in the village of Borden and went to train with the local football team, Borden Village FC. I saw him on Saturday afternoons and my mum had said I could stay over and go to the match on the Sunday morning.

I vaguely remember seeing my dad's final game for Gillingham. I recall that he hoisted me up onto his shoulders and carried me around the ground with him, milking the applause of a relieved and euphoric crowd. He had blue and white scarves draped around his neck. I still have one that he gave me. I was eight years old, and now, six years later I was going to see him play again.

Borden Village had won promotion the previous season to the Kent Sunday Premier Division for the first time, and there was a lot of excitement about the team's prospects, especially as they now had an ex-professional in their team. The landlord of the pub had hired the coach and promised to do the same for the rest of the season if there was enough interest for away games. The pub, the Maypole Inn, had its name blazoned across the team's blue shirts and after games it was expected that players and spectators alike went there to celebrate or to drown their sorrows.

I don't remember exactly where that first game was, but it was out in the sticks somewhere and the coach twisted and crawled along leafy Kentish lanes until eventually we came to some out of the way sport's field. When the coach parked up, I woke my dad up and carried his kitbag off the bus and into the changing rooms. I then disappeared to have a look around. My dad had told me not to stay since I guess he didn't want me bombarded by a lot of vulgar jokes and coarse language. He obviously thought I was still just a kid, but I wasn't. I was fourteen and very nearly an adult, at least I thought I was.

I walked around the edge of the huge field where the game was going to take place. Like most village playing fields it was used for cricket in the summer and football in the winter and as this was the first game of the football season the cricket square was still clearly visible. The football pitch had bright white lines which showed it had only recently been marked out. The goalposts and nets looked like they had been bought new for the season too. It was a big field and I walked slowly and sure enough, when I had been all the way round the first players were beginning to emerge from the changing rooms to warm up. I sat on a wooden bench and waited for my father to appear.

When he finally emerged he was involved in an argument with the Manager, but seeing me he gave up and came to sit next to me on the bench.

"Manager's an idiot," he informed me.

"What's up dad?" I asked.

"I'm sub," he said grumpily. My dad was the new superstar striker, the ex-professional, without doubt the best player ever to sign for Borden Village in the team's entire history. The Manager really was an idiot.

My dad sat and sulked for ten minutes or so and then suddenly got to his feet and jogged across the pitch to join in the warm up with the keeper who was doing catching practice. My dad might be the great Martin Henderson, the Martin Henderson who once saved Gillingham from relegation and played sixteen times for Brentford, but he was going to have to start the season as sub for Borden Village in the lowest league he had ever played in. I wasn't worried I figured that my dad would soon show the Manager that he was good enough for the team.

When the game kicked off my dad dutifully went and sat on the sub's bench, at the far end away from the Manager. I remained seated on the wooden seat outside the changing rooms a little back from the pitch but with a good enough view of the game since there weren't many spectators at all. There were a handful of regulars from the village pub who had come with us on the coach, the home side had only a couple of old men who had been walking their dogs and were probably only going to stay for a few minutes. Just as the whistle blew for the start, a girl who had been standing beside the pitch turned and saw my half-empty bench and decided to come over.

"Al'right if I sit here?" she asked.

"Sure," I said.

"You're the new player's son ain't you?"

"Yeah."

"The Manager's my dad." I just nodded. It probably wasn't a nice idea to tell her that her father was an idiot, so I just kept quiet. She sat down beside me and we observed the opening moments of the game. After a while she turned and looked at me.

"Don't say much do you?" This confused me since I thought we were there to watch the match, and besides I couldn't for the life of me think why she would want to talk to me. She was older than me, how much older I couldn't tell, maybe three or four years, and she was pretty too, and that combination suddenly made me feel very nervous.

"What's your name?" she wanted to know.

"Stevie." I cursed myself instantly, I should have said Steve, Stevie was a kid's name. Stevie was what my mum called me.

"I'm Helen," she told me. "Which school do you go to?"

I told her. It turned out that she was at the girl's grammar school which shared a playing field and sports facilities with mine. I was relieved that she didn't go to the school where my dad worked. Then she wanted to know what year I was in and when I told her she said that I looked older than that, which I took as a compliment. She had just started in the sixth form. How far out of my depth did I feel? Well, to put it into football terms, I was Borden Village FC and she was Manchester Fucking United. She carried on asking me questions about anything and everything. Why she was so curious about my life I don't know.

195

Anyway, if her motivation was to get through a boring football match it was working, since before I knew it the half time whistle went and the teams went back to the changing rooms for a cup of tea and a breather. It was the first game of the season and it was quite a hot day and those who had taken part in the first forty-five minutes looked shattered. There hadn't been any goals, so there was everything to play for in the second half.

Helen opened a small shoulder bag that she had brought with her and took out a can of diet coke and a packet of crisps.

"Didn't you bring anything to eat?" she asked me.

"No, I was at my dad's last night." My mum would have provided me with a snack of some sort, but my dad hadn't thought to.

"You can share mine if y'like." She offered me the crisps and I took one. She opened the can of drink, took a quick sip and passed it to me. I drank also. Then I noticed my dad emerge from the changing rooms still with his tracksuit top on, shin pads in hand. He came over to the bench.

"The Manager's still an idiot," he said. "Who's your girlfriend?"

"This is Helen," I told him, "she's the Manager's daughter."

He just laughed and jogged out onto the pitch to do a bit of warming up. Obviously the Manager had told him that he would be brought into the game soon. I took another sip of diet coke and passed the can back to the girl. The other players returned to the pitch so that the match could get under way again.

After ten minutes or so my dad was finally given his chance. When I saw him take the field I clapped loudly hoping to inspire him. I knew he hadn't played a real game for a few years and I was afraid that he might make a fool of himself, and therefore me. I needn't have worried within a few minutes he broke free of the defence and nonchalantly rounded the keeper to score the game's first goal. A few minutes later he scored a second direct from a free kick from the edge of the box. By the end of the match he had scored all four in a four-nil victory. I was euphoric. After the coach returned to Borden everyone piled into the pub to celebrate and my dad held court sitting at the bar telling stories about his time as a professional. I was given a coke and some crisps and wandered out into the beer garden. I found Helen there sitting at one of the wooden tables on her own enjoying the sunshine. I went over to sit with her. I offered her some crisps and she smiled at me. She had a nice smile.

Half an hour later my mum arrived to collect me. My dad was still at the bar and well on the way to getting drunk when I went to say goodbye. He said he'd see me on Saturday and I returned to the beer garden where my mum was talking to Helen.

"Are you coming next week?" I asked the Manager's daughter.

"Maybe," she replied.

In the car on the way back into town I told my mum about the game and about my dad's four goals. She feigned interest for a while, and then as we turned into Homewood Avenue she turned to look at me.

"I like your girlfriend," she laughed.

"She's not my girlfriend," I said. I should be so lucky.

TWO

On Monday at the end of morning school I wolfed down my sandwiches as usual and went out onto the field with my friends to have a game of football. We piled up our black blazers as goal posts and a frantic match soon got underway. I wasn't really that good at football, but I felt inspired by my father's four goals the previous day and scored myself after only a few minutes. As I turned to celebrate I was surprised to see a small group of sixth formers from the girls' grammar school standing close by. They were easily recognisable as sixth formers because they didn't have to wear a uniform like the younger girls. I realised that Helen was among them. She looked good in jeans and a white T-shirt, her long blonde hair glowing with the sun behind her. She smiled at me. No one else saw. I smiled back and watched her walk away with her friends.

*

The following Saturday afternoon my dad came to pick me up. The week had dragged slowly by. Apart from that one brief glimpse on Monday I hadn't seen Helen again. It wasn't normal for sixth formers to be out on the playing field with the younger kids since they were allowed to go into town at lunchtime.

My dad took me to Mc Donald's as all the other divorced dads did with their kids on Saturday lunchtimes. The place was full. There was nowhere else to go really, not in our town. After we had finished eating, we went to the park and sat on a bench and watched the dads with younger children play on the swings and slides. We didn't talk much, my dad didn't really know what to say to me I guess. He asked how school was going and how football training was and that sort of thing. I told him that I wasn't really that great at football and that I probably wouldn't make it to be a professional like he had been. He said not to worry since studies were the most important thing, not football. I didn't have the heart to tell him that my studies weren't going well either. I hadn't been chosen for the grammar school at eleven and I wasn't particularly good at anything. I didn't cause trouble and I did all my homework on time and generally kept my nose clean.

Saturday night I slept over again. We watched Match of the Day together and then I went to bed. I lay awake most of the night, thinking about Helen and hoping she was going to be at the ground the next morning.

I awoke to find a thin mist had crept over the village during the night and I worried that it might rain and that Helen might not fancy watching a football match in bad weather. I had a bowl of cereals in my dad's tiny kitchen watching the sky through the dirty window and trying to convince myself that the sun was going to come out. There was a last minute panic as my dad packed his kitbag and couldn't remember where he had left his shin pads, but eventually I managed to find them in a plastic bag at the back of his wardrobe and so we hurried off up the road to the ground.

Borden Village FC play their home games at a place called Borden Playstool which also doubles as the cricket pitch. It's a pretty place, somewhat hidden away in a dip and surrounded by cherry orchards. As we walked down the hill to the ground I saw that the mist was concentrated in the bowl where the pitch was. I hoped the game wouldn't be cancelled. Looking up at the sky I saw that the sun was desperately trying to break through and chase the mist away.

My dad was the last to arrive and I heard a series of whistles and shouted abuse as he entered the home dressing room. Looking around the club house I was relieved to see Helen sitting on a plastic chair by the little kitchen. She was reading a book but she looked up when she heard the commotion of my father's entrance and saw me. She smiled. I liked it when she smiled at me. I went over to stand by her.

"Hi," I said. "What y'reading?"

"Nothing, some Shakespeare for school, that's all. I was waitin' for you."

"Wanna go for a walk 'round the ground?" I suggested.

"Okay then," she said and she got to her feet and stuffed her Shakespeare into her bag. "I brought you a snack for half time."

We set off from the clubhouse around the edge of the playing field. The grass was wet and the cobwebs shone despite the mist. We walked along the side of the ground by the cherry orchard.

"Saw you at school on Monday," I told her.

"I know I came to look for you."

"You did?"

"Yeah. I told my friends I'd met this cute guy and they wanted to see you."

"I expect they said I was just a kid right?"

"Well, they said you were young, but they said you were cute too."

I laughed and blushed at the same time.

By the time we'd finished our lap of the Playstool the players had come out to warm up. The sun was slowly burning away the mist. It was going to be the perfect morning for football. My dad jogged over to tell me that he was going to be playing from the start this time.

"Maybe your girlfriend's old man isn't such an idiot after all," he said as he turned to go back to the warm up. We carried a wooden bench out of the clubhouse and sat together through a dismal first half. We were the only ones watching although a few more turned up later. Borden Village were losing 1-0 and it was a bad-tempered and scrappy game. Helen gave me some biscuits she had brought with her and we shared a can of diet coke. If the first half had been bad then the second was terrible and we lost all interest in the game and talked about music instead. The visitors scored a second and that was how it ended. There would be no talk of winning the league in the pub today. My dad had a quiet game and came off moaning about the lack of service.

Helen and I sat out in the beer garden as the sun was now out. Eventually, my mum turned up to pick me up.

"See you next week," I called out to the girl.

"Maybe," she called back.

*

I didn't see Helen at all during the following days and I worried that she might not come again. It was a cold week of strong winds and slanting rain signalling that winter was well and truly on the way. My mum wasn't so sure that I should go to the match on Sunday, but fortunately things were brighter on Saturday and I managed to convince her that I should stay at my father's place and travel with him to the match. She didn't protest too much, I think she appreciated the freedom to do what she liked on a Saturday night after so many years. Perhaps she went out with some friends for a few drinks in town, maybe she had a secret lover that only came over when I wasn't there. More than likely, knowing my mum, she just cuddled up on the sofa under a blanket and watched some terrible old weepy film.

Sunday morning we boarded the coach to venture once more off into the wilds of Kent in search of some unknown playing field out in the middle of the marshes. When I got on I quickly scanned the faces of those already there looking for Helen but I couldn't find her. In desperation I checked for the Manager and was relieved to see that he hadn't arrived yet. A couple of minutes later I saw them hurrying towards us from the lane to the left of the church. This must be the street where they lived. I was sitting next to my dad, who was already wriggling around to get comfortable, ready to nod off as soon as the bus was in motion, but when she got on Helen whispered for me to go sit with her. I slipped quietly from my seat and followed her a little further down the aisle. I don't think my dad even realised that I had gone and so we sat together on the coach for the first time. She sat by the window and pointed out interesting things as we crawled along the country lanes towards the M20, I couldn't have cared less, I was happy just to look at her and to hear her voice after a whole week of missing her.

Somewhere down the M20 it began to drizzle and it didn't stop for the rest of the morning. Fortunately, Helen had a small umbrella in her bag and we were able to stand together under a big tree to watch the match. We were so close we were almost touching. We took turns to hold the umbrella, since it gave you arm-ache if you held it too long. At half time she surprised me with a flask of hot tea and we held it in our freezing hands and sipped at it. It was a good job that Borden Village were back on song that day, as it would have been a really miserable trip, had it ended in defeat. They won 3-1 my dad scoring the first and creating the other two.

*

That week, I got my first call up to the school team. I think I had finally worn down the teacher who coached the team after over two years of never missing training. Also the team had had a very poor start to the season and a number of the star players had lost interest in playing for what they called a bunch of losers. I was delighted to play, of course, and spent a nervous couple of days after the team sheet was put up waiting for the match which was Wednesday after school against, would you believe, the school where my dad worked. When I rang him up to tell him he was delighted, but warned me that his team were very good.

I played my first proper game of football. I was nervous as anything, but fortunately my dad was right, his team were miles better than us, and so I hardly had a touch, alone up front as I was. After about a quarter of an hour I noticed a girl walking across the playing field from the girls' grammar school towards the pitch. As she got nearer I noticed the long blonde hair blowing in the wind and realised that is was Helen. How had she known I was playing football? Now I was really nervous. I started to run about a bit rather than just stand on the half way line so that it appeared that I was actually involved in the game in some way. I think I touched the ball twice in the first half and both times I lost it straight away. It was lucky that there were no subs and so I couldn't be taken off. My mother arrived at half time as she had promised she would. She ignored my father and went to stand with Helen.

We had conceded five goals in the first half and our opponents added another couple at the beginning of the second and then they eased up a bit. I don't know how it happened, but right at the end of the game I found myself chasing a long hopeful ball played over the top. Somehow it bounced over one of their defenders and suddenly I was clean through on goal. It had never occurred to me that I might ever have the chance to score a goal and now without really meaning to I was left with just the keeper to beat. I panicked. I just kicked the ball as hard as I could straight at the keeper who had rushed out towards me. It cannoned off his chest and hit me straight in the face knocking me to the ground. I lay in the mud, half dazed. When I picked myself up I was surprised to find my team mates all around me, congratulating me on scoring. Apparently, the ball had looped back over the keeper and into the goal. And so we lost 7-1 to my dad's school, and I got the one.

At the final whistle Helen waved to me and set off back across the playing field towards the school gates. I couldn't just let her leave without saying anything to her. I ran after her, ignoring my mum and dad. I soon caught up with her and tugged at her arm.

"Thanks for coming to watch," I panted.

"That's al'right. Your dad told mine in the pub last night that you was playing. Thought I'd come see if you was any good."

"Sorry to disappoint you,"

"You didn't get the ball much, but at least you scored."

"That was just luck."

"Next time you'll get a better one."

"Will I see you on Sunday?"

"Maybe."

I watched her walk away towards the gates where her mum was waiting to pick her up, and then I went to get changed.

THREE

The Sunday match was played at Borden. When my dad woke me I looked out of the window and realised that it was pouring with rain. My dad wanted to ring my mum and get her to come pick me up, but I convinced him to let me go to the match and sit in the clubhouse. I didn't think it was very likely that Helen would be there, but I had to go just in case.

We arrived late since my dad had rescued his best boots from the plastic bag where he had left them the previous week and found them covered in a layer of white furry mould. He insisted on cleaning them in the kitchen sink, soaking them in hot water until they steamed. My mum would have had a fit if he had done something like that in her sink.

Helen was sitting on a plastic chair near the little kitchen reading her Shakespeare again. She was studying English Lit, French and History for A Level and she said it was a lot of hard work, a lot of reading. I'd done my homework on Friday after school to get it out of the way, not that I'd had much to do. I didn't think I'd be doing A Levels, it seemed like too much work to me.

As it was pouring with rain we didn't take a bench outside to sit and watch the match, instead we stayed inside, sitting on plastic chairs near the kitchen and talking quietly together. The players briefly reappeared at half time smothered in mud and shivering with cold. The game was goal-less my father told me. Helen and I helped pour out cups of tea for everyone and then we were alone once more for the second half.

At some stage I asked her how many hours of homework she had to do each night after school and she said normally three or four. I was scandalised. How could anyone do three or four hours of homework a night? She said that she normally went to the library after school and did an hour or so of homework there until her mum came to get her and then she would work in her bedroom after tea until she got everything done. I didn't have the heart to tell her that I usually only did ten to fifteen minutes homework when I got home from school, as I waited for my mum to come home from work.

We were interrupted by the unexpected arrival of my father.

"Got sent off," he mumbled. "The ref's an idiot." My dad went into the changing room to get a shower. His getting sent off was terrible news, it meant that he would be banned from playing and I might miss a game or two. It took my dad less than five minutes to get showered and changed.

"Come on son, we're outta here."

"What?"

"Say goodbye to your girlfriend, I wanna get away before the Manager gets 'ere."

I got to my feet and said goodbye to Helen. She smiled briefly and reached for her bag and the Shakespeare. We hurried away from the ground like scurrying rats. Back at his house I asked my dad what he had got sent off for.

"Don't think the ref liked something I said," was all he would admit.

*

Monday after school I went to the library and found Helen sitting alone at a table in the reference section. She didn't seem surprised to see me and whispered a quick 'hi' as I sat down opposite her. I made a big fuss about extracting my books from my bag, as if I really was there to do something meaningful and then I sat chewing the end of my pencil watching Helen do her work. After an hour she looked up from her books and gave me a little smile.

"Time to go she whispered."

We packed our things away and I waited with her in the porch until her mum arrived to pick her up.

"D'you want a lift Stevie?" offered Helen's mum.

"No thanks. I just live around the corner." I watched Helen climb into the car and stood there as it drove off and out of sight in the direction of Park Road. Then I set off for home which was in Albany Road. We lived above the hairdressing salon where my mum worked, in a cramped flat that the owner of the salon rented to my mother, as part of her monthly wages. It was okay I guess, nice and central. Near to the park and not too far from my school.

I called my dad when I got home, before my mum came upstairs from the salon. My plan was to convince him that we ought to watch the game next Sunday even though he wouldn't be eligible to play. I figured if I rang him every night after school I might break him down by the weekend. He wasn't in a good mood. Bad day at work I guess. He told me that the Manager had called him Sunday night and had a go at him over the phone. Apparently Borden Village had lost one-nil and the Manager blamed my dad for the defeat. My dad firmly rejected my idea of going to the game on Sunday and said he wanted to keep a low profile until his ban was over.

The next evening after school I went to the library again. This time I had a bit of homework to do, so after a brief spell of watching Helen work I started on my own stuff. I was surprised that after a while I needed to look something up, so I went and found a book. Normally I would just have fudged the answer and not cared that it was obviously wrong, but here in the reference section there was no excuse to give an inaccurate answer to anything. The hour flew past and when Helen announced it was time to go I quickly brought my essay to a close and then stared at it in disbelief. It was easily the longest piece I had ever written, but more importantly I knew it was good, at least by my standards.

Her mum came to pick her up. I told her that I wouldn't be at the library the following night as I had a football match over on the Isle of Sheppey. She wished me luck and we parted. I went home to nag my dad about Sunday, although I was beginning to realise that it was pointless.

The football match the following evening after school was the second and last of my fledgling football career. This time the teacher had a substitute at his disposal and used him to replace me at half time, we were 4-0 down by then and at the end it was seven. I played so badly that I didn't even bother to go to training again after that, besides I liked being in the library with Helen even though it meant I had to do homework.

I was surprised the next day at school when the teacher handed me back the essay I had done in the library and had given me an A. I was so shocked that if I hadn't been sitting down I would have fallen over. My friends looked at it in disbelief and then wanted to know who had done it for me. I can honestly say that it was the start of a new attitude on my part and I stopped drifting through life towards what I had always assumed would be academic failure. From then on I began to take an interest in what was being said in class, and was surprised that sometimes what was going on was in fact quite interesting. I did my homework in the library like the grammar school kids and found that my marks steadily began to improve in all areas. Also, if I had a problem I didn't understand I would show it to Helen and she in very patient whispers would explain it to me.

*

When my dad's two match ban for foul and abusive language towards a referee ended we were able to return to football on Sunday mornings. Borden Village had lost both games without him and hadn't managed a goal in his absence. If he thought that the Manager had forgiven him or was desperate for a goal he was wrong, and he found himself amongst the substitutes. Had my father known in advance then I think he wouldn't have bothered to go at all, but he was there now, on the Isle of Thanet with no way home except the team bus, and so he paced the touchline fuming. Helen and I watched the match sitting on the bonnet of someone's car, as the edge of the pitch was so close to a road. At half time Borden Village was losing 1-0 and had been a bit of a shambles. What had happened to the lively team of a few weeks before I wondered? All confidence seemed to have gone.

My dad continued to prowl the touchline like a caged tiger waiting to maul the bastard who had put him behind bars. Every now and then he would stop and give the Manager an evil glare, but the Manager never seemed to look in his direction. Eventually with his team heading for obvious defeat, Helen's dad saw sense and brought his star striker into the game. The effect was instant and dramatic. I had been worried that my father might be too angry, too pumped up and that he would get himself sent off again, but of course he had once been a professional and so he channelled everything that was pissing him off into sheer determination. The first time the ball was played into his feet he twisted away from his marker and burst through on goal. He rounded the keeper with ease and smashed the ball into the goal so hard I thought he might break the net then he went over and started kicking the post as if it had done him an injury. Luckily his team mates dragged him away before he broke his foot or the post. Then he did it again, almost a carbon copy of the first goal. This time he left the post alone and just stood, chest puffed out staring at the Manager until his team mates dived on him. That was

207

enough to win the game, just two flashes of brilliance from a very angry man.

My dad slept all the way back and I sat next to Helen. She said she felt tired and she rested her head on my shoulder and we stayed like that all the way home. In the pub my dad happily held court at the bar, reliving his goals and with everyone laughing at his telling of his assault of the goal post. The Manager was standing beside him laughing and I hoped that all was well between them again. I didn't want my dad and Helen's dad at each other's throats. It was cold outside so Helen and I sat in the corner out of the way and I looked into her blue eyes as she talked about something that I wasn't really interested in, but I wouldn't have wanted to be anywhere else, for anything in the world. Maybe you think I was beginning to fall in love with Helen, but that wouldn't be true. I had been in love with her from the first time we had met. The big thing that worried me was how she felt about me in return. Did she see me as just a friend, someone to pass a few hours with on a Sunday morning? Someone who studied with her in the library after school? I had no way of knowing. I knew she liked me, but liking and loving someone were very different, very, very different.

*

My dad went on an explosive goal-scoring spree over the next few weeks, grabbing the headlines in the local paper and propelling Borden Village FC up towards the top of the league table. The Playstool was blessed with more and more supporters for home games and the travelling coach to away games was nearly full every time, and this despite the cold weather as Christmas approached. Helen and I watched the games wrapped in scarves and hats and wearing big coats, warming our hands over half time tea or sometimes soup, if her mum had thought it might be especially cold.

In the last game before the two-week Christmas break, my dad scored a last minute winner and the team went top of the league.

FOUR

I couldn't believe my school report when I got it on the last day of term. I usually got a collection of Cs and Ds with a "could try harder" undertone to the teachers' comments, but my marks had all risen. I had three As and the rest were all Bs. My mum almost died of shock when I showed her, in fact she sat down at the kitchen table and cried and then told me to ring my dad. He was pleased too. I rang Helen and told her. She had straight As in all her subjects as usual she said, but she was pleased for me and said I needed to keep up my efforts and change the Bs into As for next time.

I saw Helen in the Maypole on New Year's Eve. It had taken some doing but I'd managed to convince my mum that she should go out with her friends, which meant I got dumped on my dad, just as I had hoped. I rang Helen and told her I'd be in the pub and she said that her parents always went there on New Year's Eve and that she would go along with them.

We arrived at the pub to find it packed, I think everyone in the village was there. It took me a while to find Helen, but when I did she followed me to an out of the way corner and we spent the rest of the night chatting and listening to music. At midnight we found her parents and my dad and toasted together and sang auld lang syne and when we were alone again hidden away, she hugged me and wished me a happy new year and a happy new century, seeing as it was now the long-awaited year 2000. I hugged her back and wondered if I should kiss her, but they started playing Prince's 1999 and everyone around us started dancing and so we joined in.

*

Borden Village FC made an embarrassing start to the new millennium losing 5-0 at home to the bottom club. My dad said it was the worst game he'd ever played in. They would have to find their feet again quickly or all hope of winning the league would be gone. But they didn't. January was a terrible month with only a single point gained from their three matches. The first week in February they were knocked out of the cup by a team from a lower division and things were not looking good.

It was the change in the weather that brought a change in fortune for the team. The days became drier and the pitches weren't so heavy and Borden's passing game could once again flourish. My dad returned to the score sheet too and they began to move back up towards the top of the league once more.

Helen and I were able to sit outside and watch the games again, rather than pass the time in dingy clubhouses or under trees. We always walked around the pitch before the kick off, home or away. I liked the away games best because we sat together on the coach.

*

The football season began to draw to a close, with the slow approach of spring. Borden Village FC had risen to second in the table and was just one point behind the leaders going into the final game. As fate would have it the fixture list had the two top teams paired together in the last match, with Borden the home side, needing a win to take the title, whilst for the visitors a draw would do.

I had never seen the Playstool so packed. It was a beautiful morning and the cherry trees around the ground were in full blossom. Helen and I walked around the ground as usual, but for the final game we were going to have to stand. There were so many people we wouldn't have been able to see from our bench outside the clubhouse. We stood at the end of the line of watchers behind the rope to keep spectators back from the pitch.

The visitors, who would be champions if they didn't lose packed their defence and played for a draw. It was a frustrating match to watch with our team throwing everything forward and the other side just sitting back and defending. At half time it was still goal-less and I wondered what Helen's dad could come up with to change things around. In all honesty there wasn't too much more he could ask of his players, they had worked their socks off.

The second half took much the same pattern as the first, but then, with ten minutes left, the visitors did the unthinkable and scored a goal. There were loud groans from the spectators and you could see the heads of the Borden players drop, but with the title slipping from their grasp the Blue-Skinned Gods raised themselves for one final onslaught.

With about five minutes plus injury time remaining in the season, my dad wriggled free of his marker and got a shot in on the turn from the edge of the box. The keeper reacted well and pulled off a good save, but he couldn't hold it and my father gratefully netted the rebound. The crowd went wild. Helen and I jumped for joy. I now firmly believed that my dad would be able to win the game in the remaining few minutes, I felt it was his destiny, just as it had been to save Gillingham from being relegated to the Conference back in 1993.

Borden Village swarmed forward like never before, and every time they managed to get the ball into the box there were gasps of excitement from those watching, but the visitors somehow managed to hold out. I saw the referee check his watch and realised that there was maybe the chance for one last attack. My dad picked up the ball in the centre of the pitch and began to run towards the heart of the opposition defence. They backed off from him thinking he would pass the ball, but he had other ideas and with a sudden change of pace he surged through the middle and into the box. The keeper rushed at him and I thought my dad would just slip the ball under him or something, but he didn't, he decided to take the ball round the goalie and walk it into the empty net. There was a stunned silence and then it turned quickly to pandemonium. We cheered with all our might. Borden Village had won the league. Helen hugged me to her and we jumped up and down for a bit. When we stopped jumping I realised that we were locked together and that our lips were almost within touching distance. And I did it. I leaned forward and I kissed her. I'd wanted to do it for so long, but I'd been scared of ending our friendship. And now I'd done it. We broke the kiss and stood kind of stunned just looking at each other. She must have read the look of distress on my face because she gave me a smile.

"What took you so long?" she whispered, and she locked her lips back onto mine and we kissed again, longer than the first time.

Also by Kelvin Hughes

THE LAST LORRY

Madrid. March 1939.

The final hours of the Spanish Republic.

As the doomed Spanish capital prepares to surrender after two years of stubborn resistance, one final mission remains. A lorry, disguised as an ambulance, must leave the city and head south to the port of Alicante, where a ship is waiting to take its valuable secret cargo to South America. The lorry's cargo is so important that the victorious rebels will stop at nothing to capture it.

The person given this unenviable task is a young Captain, Daniel Miller Gonzalez, a man who has proved his loyalty to the legitimate Government of Spain on battlefields across the Iberian Peninsula. Together with his lifelong friend Fernando, an English nurse, and the driver of the lorry, Dani tries to outwit the advancing forces of General Franco in a dangerous game of cat and mouse along the last remaining route south out of Madrid. He knows that this final corridor of escape is closing in on him and that every moment is vital, but they can only travel along the back roads and at night as Rebel aircraft are out hunting for them during the daytime.

The man entrusted with the task of hunting down the last lorry is the ruthless Captain Roberto Ruiz Roman, a brutal and sadistic expert in extracting information and sniffing out 'Reds.' And, as General Franco himself has said "better Dead than Red." Captain Ruiz has the entire rebel war machine at his disposal for this final wartime mission, and he is not a man accustomed to failure.

This is a story of supreme loyalty, of courage when all hope is lost, and, ultimately, of betrayal.

Follow On Facebook: Kelvin Hughes - Writer

Printed in Poland
by Amazon Fulfillment
Poland Sp. z o.o., Wrocław